The LANGUAGE *of*
HOUSEPLANTS

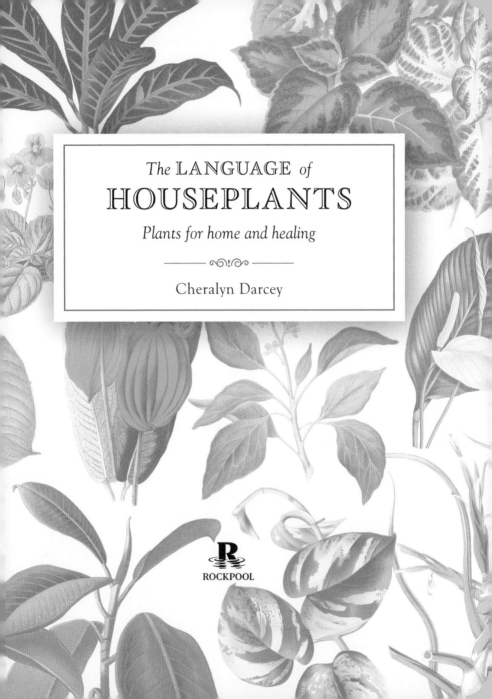

The LANGUAGE of
HOUSEPLANTS

Plants for home and healing

—— ⌒∾!∾⌒ ——

Cheralyn Darcey

R

ROCKPOOL

A Rockpool book
PO Box 252
Summer Hill
NSW 2130
Australia

www.rockpoolpublishing.co
www.facebook.com/RockpoolPublishing
Follow us! **f** 🄾 rockpoolpublishing
Tag your images with #rockpoolpublishing

ISBN: 978-1-925924-39-8

First published in 2020
Copyright text © Cheralyn Darcey 2020

Edited by Katie Evans
Design by Jessica Le, Rockpool Publishing
Typesetting by Sara Lindberg, Rockpool Publishing

A catalogue record for this
book is available from the
National Library of Australia

Printed and bound in China
10 9 8 7 6 5 4 3

We may think we are nurturing our garden,
but of course it's our garden that is really nurturing us.

JENNY UGLOW

For my sister Jane Darcey,
apart from being a best friend and wonderful sister,
you are one of the loveliest humans I know!

THANK YOU

This book of houseplants, like all my work is close to my heart. It took me years to research and years to write, and I deeply appreciate the support and encouragement of those who made it possible.

It is with much joy that I thank my family, friends and the supportive team at Rockpool Publishing who were there when it mattered most and helped my dream to become a reality.

Immeasurable thanks and love to every one of you who I have met online and in person and with whom I share my passion for nature, gardening and the botanical world.

I have adored our conversations and blossoming friendships over the years, and I greatly appreciate the wonderful support you have given my work.

Thanks to those of you who are holding this book now – by doing so, you are helping me to continue my work with the botanical world now and into the future. I hope this book brings each one of you the bouquet of love, happiness and insight that you are looking for.

Thank you all for keeping me growing.

Bunches of love,
Cheralyn
www.cheralyndarcey.com

CONTENTS

TAB. II.

 is a footnote reference

Philodendron eximium. Schott.

INTRODUCTION

LIVING WITH PLANTS AND THEIR ENERGY

There is no such thing as a 'houseplant'. The botanical specimens of lush green foliage that we have invited inside to share our spaces are simply plants that are found in the wild – the cave entrance- and cliff dwellers, the rainforest understory- and the filtered shade lovers – living in somewhat similar conditions as those in our lounge rooms and offices, shopping malls and hotels.

While we may be drawn to living with houseplants because they are beautiful and decorative, they each hold therapeutic energetic qualities that can be shared with us. Plants purify the air, support us emotionally, lift our moods, calm our minds, inspire productivity and help us heal, by just being there. Every plant can achieve all of these things, yet each type will garner particular and specific strengths. Through the study of traditional uses, botanical history and various plant modalities, I offer this collection of plants and their meanings in order to give you a starting point for your own explorations.

'The Language of Plants' has been a decades-long undertaking of mine and aims to explore not only the basis of why we are drawn to certain plants, but how we can better harness this natural energy for a more focused approach to improving our lives. This book details 44 popular houseplants that I am currently living with and explains the meanings of the plant names, the plants' qualities and botanical histories, so that you may better understand your own indoor plants, why you are drawn to them, and perhaps find others that you can invite into your space (based on the energies they possess to enhance your own life).

So, if you are feeling blue, for example, there could a succulent just for you, to brighten your day with joyful bursts of energy as it sits happily on your coffee table. Perhaps a calmer atmosphere in your office would be so very welcome, and here in this book you will find just the right potted plant or fern to support and to soothe those in your workspace. The overall good-vibe energy that plants contain and share is undeniable, but I invite you to come a little deeper into their world and listen carefully to exactly what each is saying and sharing.

Just like you, plants need physical care: water, food and someplace to live that they like. But they also need to be connected to those around them. Love your houseplants, learn about them and understand them, and I promise you they will love you back, their energy will be stronger, and you and everyone around you will benefit. With each entry in this book I have shared ways to care for your plants, along with my tips for a happy and healthy plant, to help you grow a thriving bond.

Bunches of happiness,
Cheralyn

HOW TO USE THIS BOOK

The Language of Houseplants is your guide to the meanings of the plant names and how to care for a popular cross-section of houseplants. The book also provides information to help you select the perfect plants for you and understand how these plants can benefit you specifically.

If you have a plant and want to understand its meanings, I would suggest you look it up in the section titled 'A Collection of Houseplants'. There, along with beautiful vintage illustrations of each houseplant, I have given you the main keyword that best describes the plant and the energy it will share, followed by the common name (the one that has the widest use) and then the botanical name. E.g.:

SPIRITUALITY
AFRICAN VIOLET
Saintpaulia spp.

Next, I've included a few more meanings that are ascribed to the plant. You can use these meanings to help you enhance your space and fill it with the plant's energy, to share the meaning if gifting the plant to another, or to imbue a celebration or event with the sentiment attached to these meanings. After this, I've included suggestions on how and where the plant could best be used and shared. E.g.:

MEANINGS
protection, direction, self-confidence, higher learning

USES

African Violets will lift the energy of any space and bring illumination to those who feel they are overburdened or lost. A great plant to have in areas of homes and work spaces where learning or creative pursuits are taking place. The plant will also help boost self-confidence. Give to another to say 'You will find a way', 'I believe in you' or 'Good luck'.

A botanical profile of each plant further helps you understand its heritage and qualities. E.g.:

PROFILE

An African Violet is a rather small plant that grows almost hugging the earth. The down-covered leaves splay out to form a circle of greens (etc.)

You need to know how to care for your plant – not only to keep it alive but to better understand its characteristics. I've then included a specific gardening care guide that includes watering requirements, containing, feeding and position information, along with extra advice on propagating and grooming your plant.

If you are looking for general indoor plant advice, troubleshooting and tips, then hop into the 'General Houseplant Care' section. Here you will find help and resources, ideas and inspiration.

Should you already have an occasion, personal challenge or need for your living and working spaces, then turn to the last section of this book for lists of meanings, birthday months and more information that could further help you select the perfect plant for you, your space or a loved one.

Further, the toxicity levels of all plants in this book have been listed, but these levels are a general guide only and will be affected by individual circumstances. Humans and pets can also have allergies to certain plants, and so best practice is to have your plants out of reach of small children and animals.

LEARNING THE LANGUAGE OF HOUSEPLANTS

When we bring a houseplant into our lives, we are inviting another living thing to share space with us, which will have an individual energy that can affect us. Although this energy is not visible, it can be understood by observing the characteristics plants display, and the way they interact with their environment and those they share it with.

Much like the meanings in my affirmation cards *The Language of Flowers*, plants also have an individual meaning to describe their energy – an energy that can enhance our lives and spaces. This language is based on 'The Doctrine of Signatures', an ancient memory aid used in herbal medicine, in aromatherapy and other flower-based therapies, to understand the properties of a plant based on its individual appearance, characteristics and environment.

While we may benefit from understanding this energy, we must respect that it is primarily there for the plant itself. Most of us are perhaps more drawn to the flowers and qualities of angiosperms, (flowering plants). Perfumed and aromatherapy items created with flowers change and support us through our emotions and so have a therapeutic effect. The flowers of various plants also feature in herbal medicines, teas, cosmetics and so on, and all have proven, or at least long-held, experiential benefits.

It is relatively easy to understand the language of flowers. For example, we know that roses represent love, daisies represent happiness and lilies grief (well, actually, support). To learn the language of all plants is not difficult and there was a time when humans were still hunters and gatherers, and understanding this language sometimes meant the difference between life and death. In our modern world, we have simply forgotten this language.

We are attracted to flowers because they give us something, whether it is an uplifting feeling when placing a bunch of daisies in our office, or calming down at the end of a hectic day with a cup of chamomile tea. We just gravitate towards them. This is because they share benefits with us that we feel we want. Like the pollinators (bees, birds and animals), we are more likely to gather, plant and look after angiosperm plants. They will survive, and they will carry their line forward if they are working in synergy with those who share their spaces. Flowers are the reproductive parts of blooming plants and so they employ different energetic qualities, usually strongly, so that they may attract pollinators, and us.

Look a little deeper, work a little more closely with the botanical world, as a guardian of plants, a gardener (outdoors or in), and the benefits are limitless. The foliage may provide protection and support for the plant, but, more importantly, the leaves assist with the manufacture of food for the plant, help with the evaporation of water and support the exchange of gases between the plant and the atmosphere. The root system, the trunk, stems, seeds, fruits and all the rest of a plant will also have separate functions and, again, all give indications to the overall energies and so indicate the meanings of the plant.

While you read through this book, I want you to listen to the descriptions and needs of each and take yourself to their original environments so that you can hear their language. By doing this, the subtle energies that each emits will become stronger for you and much easier to understand.

Selecting the Right Plants For You

Houseplants have found their way into my life in the same way they have probably done so in yours. Some have been gifted, others left behind or found in places I have moved through, and many have been purchased or created via propagation from a desire to have the particular plant in my life. The houseplant might have made me feel something when I saw it. The energy of the plant reached out and I was calmed and soothed, or my heart skipped a little beat in excitement as my spirits lifted. I have liked how I have felt in the presence of the plant and so I have wanted to live with it in my space.

On the surface, this is how to select the right plant for you. It feels good, it feels right, it's here, or given to you so must be meant for you. While there is nothing wrong with this response, and you should trust your feelings as they do connect with and reveal the energy of plants, bear in mind that the plants are living organisms and they have needs just like you. For example, while you could go and live at the North Pole or in Death Valley, you would need a lot of additional requirements to do so. An unaccustomed environment poses extra needs. Plants are no different.

If you wish to grow sunflowers indoors, you are going to have a tough time. They need full sun all day and a lot of room. Each plant has requirements and I have shown you in this book what they are. If you go away for weeks at a time, a rainforest plant such as a Bird's Nest fern that requires its soil to always be moist may not be for you, unless you can install a constant water supply. If your office is a cold, dark dungeon then perhaps only the Devil's Ivy will stand a chance.

Some think that only those with the mystical 'green thumb' can keep houseplants alive, let alone looking as lush and beautiful as we would desire. I don't agree with this. Gardening is a learned skill and one that is, I believe, never completely mastered by anyone. It is a continual learning experience, as organic as nature itself. Those who appear to be 'the best' at it simply spend a little over the basic time needed for whatever their form of garden requires. In this book I will share with you the basic needs of each of the listed plants and I'll also give you suggestions on going a little further in understanding where they are from and what you can do to emulate their natural environments (only for the plants that *can* adapt to living as 'house' plants).

Finding out the meanings of each plant and the energy that it shares is an important layer to selection, but so is selecting the plant for the place you wish for it to live.

Gifting Plants to Others

Most of the houseplants that find an early grave are unfortunately those gifted by well-meaning friends and family. Often purchased because they are in flower and look pretty, they are sometimes not suitable for the environments they are going into.

Because *The Language of Houseplants* explains the actual meanings and energies of plants, you can choose plant gifts more selectively – based on the message you would like to send and the energies that may be of benefit to the other person.

While this book lists 44 popular plants, there are of course millions more. If the plant you are thinking about is not listed here, look for the best match. Though the meaning may not be exact, it might be similar.

Whether you already know how to keep the plant alive and thriving, or find that information within this book or elsewhere, always include a card that states the following:

Common Name
Botanical Name
Position (out of drafts, good airflow, out of the reach of pets and children…)
Light (full sun, indirect, shade, dappled light…)
Water (when, how often, how…)
Feeding (when, how often, how…)

These simple starting points can ensure the plant has the best chance of survival once you gift it to another.

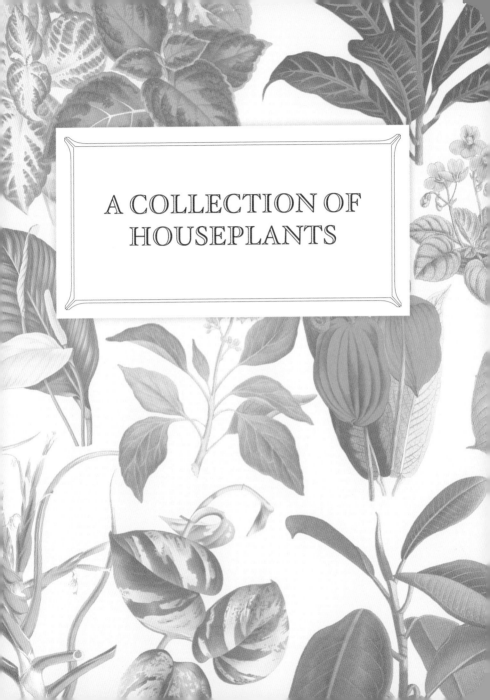

A COLLECTION OF HOUSEPLANTS

AFRICAN VIOLET

Saintpaulia spp.

Meanings
protection, direction, self-confidence, higher learning

Uses
African Violets will lift the energy in any space and bring illumination to those who feel they are overburdened or lost. A great plant to have in areas of homes and work spaces where learning or creative pursuits are taking place. The plant will also help boost self-confidence. Give to another to say: 'You will find a way', 'I believe in you' or 'Good luck'.

CARE
houseplant maintenance level = medium

Profile
An African Violet is a rather small plant that grows almost hugging the earth. The down-covered leaves splay out to form almost a circle of greens, from sage to deep emerald, surrounding, and looking as if it were presenting to the sky, a treasured cluster of delicate flowers in pinks, whites, blues, but for the most part deep and inky purples.

Native to Tanzania, south-eastern Kenya and parts of tropical eastern Africa, African Violets are a small, compact plant that are popular as a garden plant but also make a very pretty and popular houseplant. Non-toxic to humans and animals.

Container & Soil
Although they can be grown in regular potting mixes, a much better growing medium can be created with equal parts of perlite, vermiculite and peat moss, or a commercial African Violet potting mix.

Position & Light

African Violets need even, filtered light. If leaves darken, it means that your plant is not receiving enough light. A lack of light will also inhibit flowering and they also do not do well in draughty areas. They like to be in temperatures between 20–25C (70–80F) and they thrive in humid environments.

Water

African Violets are very fickle when it comes to watering and must never completely dry out or be over-watered. They need room-temperature water that has been allowed to stand for two days. Water lightly when the soil feels as though it is beginning to lose moisture. Be careful to not water leaves or flowers.

Food

There are African Violet-specific fertilisers available and these are by far the best to use. Follow the directions suggested by the manufacturer, but lightening of leaf colours usually indicates a need for feeding.

Pruning & Grooming

To encourage a longer flowering period, deadhead your plant when blooms are spent, by lightly pinching them off.

Grow More Plants

Although they can be a fickle plant to maintain, African Violets are a relatively easy plant to propagate. Remove a healthy, strong leaf from the middle of the plant, with at least a 3cm (1.5") stem. Plant it into one of the soil mixtures suggested above, and water. They can also be grown from seed or divided by cutting the crown and retaining roots in each part.

ACCEPTANCE

AIR PLANT

Tillandsia spp.

Meanings

calmness, mindfulness, clarity, communication, adaptation, ending obsession

Uses

Invite Air Plants into your life when you are in a position that cannot be changed to your liking and has become challenging to adapt to. The Air Plant will help you understand ways to enjoy new situations and surroundings as well as to enjoy yourself. They work really well in areas where children live and play, and where upsets can occur, to bring a serene and calming energy into the space. Giving an Air Plant to another will help communication between the two of you, or for them individually, and will say, 'I wish you calm', 'Congratulations (new job), (new home)'.

CARE

houseplant maintenance level = easy

Profile

An Air Plant displays fine leaves – as light as the air upon which they live – that twist from a central core to reach out and above and tentatively feel the air currents that surround them. Fragile, graceful and a little other-worldly in appearance, most blossom with even more curious-shaped flowers in the brightest crimson, magenta and purple.

Native to Mexico, southern USA, Central and South America, the Air Plant is an epiphyte, which means that it attaches itself to other plants or rocks and lives without soil. You can easily attach them to trees and larger supportive houseplants or objects. Air Plants can also be grown in containers of pebbles and they are also a popular and easy-care terrarium plant. Non-toxic to humans and animals if ingested.

Container & Soil

Air Plants can be gently planted into a pot or terrarium of pebbles, or glued or tied into place with fine cotton thread, on a tree or other plant, so they get a foothold.

Position & Light

They will need bright but indirect light. They will do well under office- or bright home lighting and can tolerate a little full sunlight each day. They prefer temperatures between about 10–30C (50–90F).

Water

A misting of water every few days is required and submersion in a container of water for thirty minutes every few weeks, or a good dousing of water every few weeks, is good for the plant. Shake off excess water and ensure good air circulation to dry.

Food

They can live happily without additional feeding, but if you wish to encourage blooming and give them a little boost, you can try a quarter strength of an orchid-, bromeliad- or houseplant-specific.

Pruning & Grooming

Trim off any brown or discoloured tips and gently pull any dead leaves on the bottom of the plant off.

Grow More Plants

Air Plants will throw off-shoots known as 'pups' that can be separated carefully by lightly pulling apart or cutting from the main plant. Replant as suggested above.

SURVIVAL

ALOE VERA

Aloe barbadensis miller

Meanings
grief, restoration, renewal, regeneration, healing

Uses
The Aloe Vera plant will calm heated energies and help those who have over-extended themselves to find better balance in their lives. It will help relieve stress and is very good in areas where people are convalescing or living with grief because it also brings emotional support and regenerative energies with it. Give to others to say, 'Get well soon', 'I hope things improve', 'I care for you' or 'I'm sorry'.

CARE
houseplant maintenance level = easy

Profile
Aloe Vera is the land-bound squid-like plant with leaves that appear as tentacles growing like a fountain from its heart. Each leaf is leathery in texture and an olive-sage green, edged with tiny serrations. Within each leaf is a clear and sticky gel that oozes generously when cut. The flower heads stand proud on long stems above the plant in red or yellow tubes that each hold a tiny bell-shaped flower.
Believed to have originated in North Africa, the earliest written record of Aloe Vera and its therapeutic applications is by the Ancient Egyptians, who used it as a medicinal aid in beauty care and in their embalming process. Mildly toxic to dogs, cats and small children if ingested.

Container & Soil
Plenty of drainage holes are a must for Aloe Vera plants, and they do well in porous pots such as those made from terracotta. Use a specific cactus/succulent potting mix or create one with half premium potting mix and half perlite.

Position & Light

Bright and constant light is vital for Aloe Vera plants. They do best outside in full sunlight but will thrive indoors in an area that has a steady and brilliant amount of light. To ensure best growth the temperature needs to be maintained above 2C (28F).

Water

The worst thing you can do to an Aloe Vera plant is to over-water it. They actually do well in soil that is left to dry out from time to time. The average watering rate is about once every two weeks, but adjust to your climate and plant.

Food

You don't really need to feed the Aloe Vera, but if it is growing a little slowly for your taste, you can give it a boost by feeding with a water-based fertiliser at half strength, every couple of weeks in the warmer months.

Pruning & Grooming

Remove leaves as required for use and any that have become damaged or spent, by cutting off at an angle with a sharp knife. Flower stalks will also need to be removed once spent and this can be done by snipping or cutting close to their base.

Grow More Plants

Aloe Vera plants produce offshoots known as 'pups'. These can be separated from the main plant by carefully cutting with a very sharp knife. Replant in one of the potting mix suggestions above. Place in a sunny spot and do not water for a week.

ARROWHEAD PLANT

Syngonium podophyllum

Meanings
new ideas, beginnings, youth, inspiration, argument, stress reduction

Uses
Arrowhead is a wonderful bedroom plant because it is known to help with sleep disorders. It can also be used in areas where meetings are held, or in general workplaces, to facilitate more open negotiations and help inspire new ideas and inspiration. It's a really good plant to invite into your life when anxiety, stress and turmoil have been present. Give to another to say, 'It is time to start again', 'I'm sorry' or 'I wish you calm'.

CARE
houseplant maintenance level = easy

Profile
The Arrowhead Plant has leaves that change their shape as they mature, beginning as an arrowhead shape and then developing into a five-fingered structure. Interestingly, the plant will have both shapes, or both immature and mature leaves, at the same time. Flowers are a cream-white lily shape much like a Calla Lily.

A native of South America and Mexico, it can be grown as a vine or a compact plant. They are a poisonous plant and toxic to humans and animals if ingested, so care should be taken when handling, plus the sap can irritate skin.

Container & Soil
The Arrowhead Plant does well in hanging baskets or pots if they are left to grow as a vine, or in a pot and pruned to deter vine development. They need to be re-potted every second Spring as they grow extensive root systems. A rich potting mix is suggested, and they do well in an African Violet mix.

Position & Light

Arrowhead plants prefer bright indirect light. If they are placed in full sun their leaves will become bleached and the plant will die. They will do best in cool to moderately warm areas between 16–24C (60–75F).

Water

Ensure that the soil is kept moist, but do not over-water. In the cooler months they will require less watering and letting them dry out a little is actually good for them.

Food

The Arrowhead Plant is a fairly heavy feeder and will benefit from a monthly liquid fertiliser in Spring and Summer, along with a specialised slow-release fertiliser

Pruning & Grooming

If you wish to grow your Arrowhead Plant as a compact houseplant, prune the growth tips and runners as soon as they appear. Vine growing plants can be left as they are.

Grow More Plants

Arrowhead Plant can very easily be grown with cuttings placed in a container of water until they develop roots. They can also be divided from sections containing viable roots and replanted.

DETERMINATION
BAMBOO PALM
Rhapis excelsa

Meanings
direction, decision, willpower, progress, action, success, movement

Uses
Choose Bamboo Palm for office spaces and areas near entrances. It helps set plans into action and keep them moving. Touch a leaf as you leave for the day to keep your willpower strong and determination high. If you can't decide on a path to take, set this plant somewhere nearby to help you. Give to another to say, 'You can do this', 'Don't give up' or 'I wish you success'.

CARE
houseplant maintenance level = easy

Profile
A slow-growing palm that is sometimes referred to as 'Lady Palm' but is usually known as 'Bamboo Palm' due to its clustered stems, which resemble the Bamboo Plant (Bambusoideae). They are an extremely efficient air purifier and coupled with their ability to tolerate low light makes them an excellent indoor plant. They have an interesting history, being originally from China, they were a prized garden feature in Japan, for Tokugawa shogunate palaces, between the years 1603–1867. Non-toxic to humans and animals.

Container & Soil
They will grow in a standard soil-based potting mixture and prefer a container only marginally larger than their root ball. You should refrain from re-potting any more than once every two to three years. Top dress with fresh potting mix at the beginning of Spring each year.

Position & Light

This plant prefers an average temperature comfortable for humans. Although it can handle lower temperatures, growth will slow down even more if it drops below 8C (46F). Bamboo Palm does not tolerate full sun and will do better in filtered light.

Water

Be careful not to over-water. Keep the body of the soil just moist with the top few centimetres (about an inch), dry for most of the year and in Winter let it dry out a little more.

Food

Bamboo Palm benefits from a full-strength feeding of a liquid fertiliser once a month. You can increase this to every second week in mid-Spring for a couple of months.

Pruning & Grooming

You need to be careful of spider mites in drier areas as these can easily take hold of this plant. Remove spent leaves gently. They will enjoy an occasional drenching outside in the rain or with a hose, to remove dust.

Grow More Plants

Look out for suckers at the base of your plant in the Spring and gently remove ensuring you have a couple of roots attached. Plant in a seed-raising or propagation soil and keep in a warm place to ensure a good start. Though challenging, they can also be propagated by seed.

WARNING
BEGONIA
Begonia spp.

Meanings

transition, warning, creativity, removal of negativity, endings

Uses

Have Begonia in your life to help dissipate negative thoughts and help your subconscious calm as well. Begonia is a very good plant to have in new homes because they clear away unwanted energies and can mark the end of one phase and the beginning of another. They also inspire creativity. Place the Begonia near the entrance to an office or home, to ward off ill-intentions. Give to another who is struggling with creative blocks or negativity, or to say, 'This must end'.

CARE

houseplant maintenance level = medium

Profile

The Begonia can be found with many different leaf styles and shapes. Various species display waxy leaves and flowers, while others have gorgeous variegations of contrasting hues that are as stunning as the blossoms they bear. Flowers are usually various pinks, reds, yellows, oranges and whites, but are found in almost any colour. There are nearly 2,000 species of Begonia and the information I have shared here is general and average for this plant. Ensure you find specific tips for your particular Begonia. They are an undershrub originating from Asia, Central and South America and Africa. Although usually a popular shade-area plant in the garden, many make very colourful houseplants as well. Highly toxic to humans and all animals if ingested.

Container & Soil

Ensure that any pot you select for your Begonia is twice the size of the root ball. Re-pot when the plant becomes root-bound in Spring. The potting mix should be half premium soil to half rich compost.

Position & Light

Most Begonias will do best in a warm area between 15–26C (60–80F), with good air circulation and indirect but bright light. Ensure that your plant is kept away from artificial heating.

Water

Soil should be kept moist but not wet. You will need to reduce watering over the cooler months of the year, but still ensure that the soil remains moist. Be very careful that the soil does not dry out.

Food

Every six months, a good slow-release fertiliser is recommended. Over Spring and Summer you may find that a liquid fertiliser every two weeks helps promote healthy growth.

Pruning & Grooming

The Begonia can be pruned at any time when they become leggy, to keep a more compact shape. You will also need to pinch off spent flowers. Tuberous Begonias will die back in the Winter and you should remove spent foliage and material at this time

Grow More Plants

Propagate by placing stem cuttings in a water-filled clear vase, until roots appear. You can also plant a single leaf with a stem cut to a point.

BIRD'S NEST FERN

Asplenium nidus

Meanings
wellness, breath, self-respect, protection, preservation

Uses
The Bird's Nest Fern grows very well in bathrooms – an excellent area to spread their energies of positivity, protection and self-respect to you as you begin and end your day. They are very good for those who are unwell and those who are recovering from accidents and sickness or trauma. Give to another to say, 'Get well soon', 'Slow down and breath' or 'Please look after yourself'.

CARE
houseplant maintenance level = easy

Profile
Large lance-shaped bright green fronds rise up around the plant, in a circle which forms a large bowl. Each frond is undivided, with slightly ruffled edges and grows up to 1.5m (5ft) in length. Overall, this tropical plant native to South-East Asia, Australia, Christmas Island, Hawaii, India, Polynesia and eastern Africa usually grows to 60 x 40cm (24 x 16") as an indoor plant, and the fronds grow to about 50cm (19.5"). Non-toxic to humans and animals.

Container & Soil
Pot in a container half the size of the plant and use a mixture of 1/3 good-quality indoor potting mix, 1/3 charcoal and 1/3 loam-based compost. Stand the pot on a tray of wet pebbles to increase humidity.

Position & Light
This fern needs constant filtered light. It will not fare well in direct sunlight or shade. Position in living areas that are a constant average temperature and that do not have draughts. Mist lightly with room temperature water every few days – they like

moderate to high humidity.

Water

The Bird's Nest Fern needs a damp soil, but you need to be careful not to let it become waterlogged. Do not water into the centre of the plant, or allow water to run into it, as this will encourage rot.

Food

From late Spring through to late Summer, feed with a liquid fertiliser made up to half regular strength, once every two weeks.

Pruning & Grooming

Fronds emerge and unfurl from the dark-brown nest-like core, and you should refrain from touching them, as they are very fragile. Re-pot in the Spring, but only when they completely fill their current container, and only go up one size in your new pot.

Grow More Plants

New plants can only be grown from the microscopic brown spores that form on the backs of mature fronds. Once formed, placed the frond in a paper bag and wait a few days until the spores fall off. Place these spores on top of a mixture of 2 litres (1/2gallon) wet peat moss mixed with ½ tablespoon ground dolomite. Cover with plastic or a dome and keep in a shaded place. Germination should occur in about 2–3 weeks.

BOSTON FERN

Nephrolepis exaltata

Meanings
luck, abundance, truth, protection, direction

Uses
Place near a front or back entranceway, to provide protection, invite luck and abundance, and ensure all those who pass into your spaces are true. Boston Fern grows exceptionally well in bathrooms, so here you can focus on your plans and directions for the day in the presence of the plant. They are also brilliant air purifiers. Give to another to say, 'I believe in you', 'I am true to you' or 'I hope you find your way'.

CARE
houseplant maintenance level = easy

Profile
A fountain of bright-green feathery fronds spray out to form a plant of up to 1m in diameter, although the usual size is about 60 x 60cm (24 x 24"). Boston Fern is sometimes known as Sword Fern and is native to most tropical areas around the world. They are a hardy plant that likes to grow in warm, humid places. This plant detests cold draughts. Non-toxic to humans and animals.

Container & Soil
Can be planted in regular containers or hanging baskets. Use one that will accommodate the root ball, with a bit of room to grow. Boston Fern grows best in an ericaceous compost such as a commercial mix suitable for roses, azaleas and camellias. But you can also create a mixture of ½ soil and ½ compost.

Position & Light
Boston Fern prefers filtered sunlight, but will tolerate light shade well. Humidity needs to be average to high to avoid fronds browning.

Water

From mid-Spring through to late Autumn the soil should be kept slightly damp at all times. Throughout the colder months let the soil dry out a little between watering.

Food

From mid-Spring to the end of Summer feed once a month with a liquid-based fertiliser at half strength.

Pruning & Grooming

Humidity needs to be kept up and so standing on a tray or saucer of moist pebbles will help, as will misting with water a few times a week throughout the warmer months. Each Spring, re-pot, trim roots, replace the soil and move up to a larger container.

Grow More Plants

Plantlets will appear on runners around the main plant. Remove those that have taken root and replant in the same method as mature plants.

CAST-IRON PLANT

Aspidistra elatior

Meanings
work, longevity, pride, self-respect, protection

Uses
This plant will encourage diligent work of the highest quality when positioned in work spaces, but particularly in retail stores, restaurants, food outlets and offices. If you are looking at progressing in your own personal career or need some workspace protection, then the Cast-Iron Plant should be placed near the door you exit to go to your work, or near or on your desk. Give to another to say, 'Good Luck' if they are job seeking, or to say, 'I wish you protection'.

CARE
houseplant maintenance level = easy

Profile
The Cast-Iron Plant features a great cluster of upright, long and leathery leaves that will curl over gently as they mature. Its dark and dull purple flowers are usually hidden by the thick foliage and appear near the level of the soil.

Native to Japan, this plant gained the name 'Cast-Iron' due to its tenacity as an indoor plant during the Victorian era. Gas lighting was introduced at this time and it killed most other houseplants. This is a plant that does well indoors and needs very little care, but will reward you with lush and faster growth if you pay it closer attention. Non-toxic to humans and animals.

Container & Soil
The Cast-Iron Plant requires a rather rich base to grow in, so a mix of 50 per cent regular potting mix with good organic compost will be best. Plant in a pot that gives a little room around the leaf base and re-pot about every three years, in Spring, if overcrowding occurs.

Position & Light

Will grow in the shade and so makes an excellent houseplant in low-light areas, but they will grow faster in areas with filtered, medium light. Humidity can be rather low and temperatures between 5–20C (41–68F) see this plant thrive.

Water

Don't over-water the Cast-Iron Plant. It detests water-logged feet. Water more frequently in the Summer months and always let the top two-thirds of the soil dry out completely between watering.

Food

Use a liquid fertiliser once every two weeks in the warmer months.

Pruning & Grooming

Remove any spent leaves by cutting away with a sharp knife. The plant does well with a top dressing of fresh soil mix as described above, early each Spring.

Grow More Plants

In Spring, you can divide the plant in clumps, ensuring that each contains a rhizome and a minimum of two leaves. These can then be replanted in the soil mix and pot size suggested above.

CHAIN OF HEARTS

Ceropegia woodii

Meanings

love, wishes, luck, fertility, home blessing, family blessing, romantic commitments

Uses

Place this plant near the front of your home to bring happy, loving blessings to all those who reside within. It will also ensure that everyone cares for each other. Creating another plant from a cutting makes an excellent gift that will bring good luck, help grant wishes and encourage fertility. The foliage could be used in wedding bouquets or decorations to ensure a strong and long union. Give this plant to another to say, 'I love you', 'Will you marry me?', 'Good luck' or 'Blessings to you'.

CARE

houseplant maintenance level = easy

Profile

The Chain of Hearts is a delightful delicate tumbling vine of tiny dark-green leaves etched with delicate white marbling. The plant does resemble little hearts spaced out along a string, hence the common names: 'Chain of Hearts' and 'String of Hearts'. It grows as a trailing vine and makes a very lovely hanging-basket plant. Flowers are small ivory coloured tube structures with a purple base.

This pretty evergreen succulent is native to South Africa, Swaziland and Zimbabwe. In its natural environment, when the nodes that grow on its stems touch soil, it will grow a new plant. Highly toxic to humans and animals if ingested.

Container & Soil

The Chain of Hearts needs to be in a hanging basket or a container with space to trail out of. Drainage is vital, so create a base of rocks/pot fragments and then top with a mix of 50 per cent premium potting soil and 50 per cent coarse sand.

Position & Light

This plant lives within the temperature range of 8–24C (46–75F) and filtered to full sun. It does best with around four hours of direct sunlight a day.

Water

Don't over-water. From mid-Spring until late Winter water lightly. The rest of the year, particularly in Winter, water only when the soil becomes almost dried out.

Food

Use a liquid fertiliser at half the recommended strength and feed every two weeks through late Spring to late Summer.

Pruning & Grooming

When tuberous growths appear along the stems, remove the whole stem and plant the tuber in a container as described above. Remove any spent leaves or stems by pinching gently.

Grow More Plants

Easy to propagate through cuttings placed in water. Once roots develop, simply plant in similar mix and pot as described above.

CHRISTMAS CACTUS

Schlumbergera truncata

Meanings
sexuality, healing, love, confidence, togetherness

Uses
Christmas Cactus is a wonderful bedroom plant because it brings people in physical relationships closer together. In living areas, it will stimulate a greater sense of affection and togetherness. It is also an incredibly powerful healer for those who may have suffered abuse, especially sexual abuse. The plant raises confidence levels and allows the heart and soul to trust in a new future. Give to another to say, 'I enjoy being with you', 'I want to be closer to you' or 'Heal well!'.

CARE
houseplant maintenance level = average

Profile
The Christmas Cactus seems to climb out of its growing position as a many-legged crustacean. The leaves are stiff and segmented, much like a crab claw, which is where its other common names – 'Crab Claw', 'Claw Cactus' and 'Crab Cacti' – come from. Flowers are bright pinks or reds and sometimes whites, and take the form of a long tube with many petals.

A native of Brazil, its common names of 'Christmas Cactus' and 'Thanksgiving Cactus' are due to the time of the year it flowers in the Northern Hemisphere. In the wild they usually grow on the bark of other trees. Non-toxic to humans and animals.

Container & Soil
Can be grown in either pots or hanging baskets. Use a peat-based soil mix that includes at least 1/3 coarse sand, to ensure free-drainage. These plants really detest getting water-logged. Do not re-pot when in flower; wait until last blossoms are spent.

Position & Light

These do well indoors in filtered light and on windowsills that receive moderate light but are not too hot. Room temperatures of 7–18C (45–65F) are best, but moving to a slightly warmer and more humid position once flower buds appear will encourage prolific flowering.

Water

When not in flower, keep the soil moist but be very careful to not over-water. Once flowering begins, water less, letting the top of the soil dry out between watering.

Food

Use a liquid fertiliser at half strength every two weeks all year, but cease feeding once flowering ends, or in Winter, and begin again in Spring or when new growth appears.

Pruning & Grooming

If you would like a thicker growth, prune the stems in Spring – this will stimulate multiple growths from the cut area. Use a very sharp knife and cut between the segments.

Grow More Plants

With a sharp knife, cut a stem with two or three segments. Lay horizontally across soil mix in a pot and water well. Let soil dry out completely between watering. Re-pot once roots have formed.

CROTON

Codiaeum variegatum

Meanings
movement, education, development, transformation, revision

Uses
Crotons help with changes – any type of changes – and they will assist you by supporting you with decisions on your path of change. The Croton can even alert you to changes you need to make. Look at the colours your plant is displaying. More green leaves than reds?: Keep going. Reds?: Perhaps stop or slow down. Give to others who are moving, changing jobs or beginning a new phase in education, or perhaps retiring.

CARE
houseplant maintenance level = challenging

Profile
Fire reds, emerald greens, pinks and reds – all these colours can be found together on any of the plant's leathery leaves. The overall effect of a mature plant can be akin to an exploding firework display. The Croton is a stunning plant that does very well in bathrooms because they enjoy staying warm and living with humidity. Male flowers are small cream-coloured and feathery; the female flowers are yellow. Crotons are native to the western Pacific Islands, Australia, Indonesia and Malaysia, and it must be noted that all parts are toxic. The seeds can actually be fatal to children and pets, so it is not suitable for all spaces. Mild irritation to adults and animals if ingested and mild skin irritation from sap contact.

Container & Soil
Grow in a rich compost-based soil mix, in a pot that gives the root ball plenty of room. The average plant will need to be re-potted about every three years. Ensure the pot has plenty of drainage.

Position & Light
Does best within the temperature range of 15–25C, (60–76F) near filtered sunlight. Ensure that humidity is rather high, but keep away from air-conditioning, heating appliances and draughts.

Water
Use room-temperature water at all times and keep the top of the soil moist. Only water into the soil; never mist the leaves. During Winter, let the top of the soil dry out between watering.

Food
From early Spring until late-Autumn (fall), feed with a liquid fertiliser every two weeks.

Pruning & Grooming
Croton can grow up to 1.5m (5ft) in the right conditions. Pruning can keep this plant compact and encourage thicker growth. Always wear gloves, as sap is toxic.

Grow More Plants
Can be successfully propagated via tip cuttings. Remove the tip of any branch containing at least three leaves, during the growing period, and ensure it is between 10–15cm (4–6") in length. The cuttings are best planted in a commercial rooting medium.

CENTRE

CROWN OF THORNS

Euphorbia milii

Meanings
unconditional love, abundance, self-forgiveness, harmony

Uses
Crown of Thorns can help people return to their true selves and explore their innermost feelings. Despite its appearance, the Crown of Thorns is very nurturing and will bring harmony to spaces by fending off negative energy and protecting all within. Give to others who may be experiencing challenges that are disrupting their sense of self. The plant will say, 'I wish you unconditional love', 'Forgive yourself' or 'I wish you peace'.

CARE
houseplant maintenance level = easy

Profile
Crown of Thorns possesses stems that produce sharp spines that jut out at right angles. They are about as long as each limb is thick and perhaps protect the latex sap within. The leaves are a bright green but only appear during growing periods and only upon the outer tips. Tiny bright red flowers rise in clusters on the stems, above the growth tips, which will repeat if sunlight is maintained. This plant is a native of Madagascar. It is said that the plant was introduced to the Middle East and perhaps the plant used to create the crown of thorns that Jesus Christ wore during his crucifixion. Highly toxic to humans and animals if sap is ingested.

Container & Soil
This plant requires very good drainage so a mix of 2/3 premium-grade potting soil to 1/3 coarse sand is ideal. Re-pot every second year in Spring.

Position & Light

Ensure your plant receives full sun throughout the day. Failure to do so will inhibit flowering. Leaves will drop if room temperature drops below 13C (55F).

Water

Allow the top 2.5cm (1in) of soil to dry out between waterings. During Winter, let the top half of the pot dry out.

Food

Every two weeks from early Spring until the beginning of Autumn (fall), feed with a liquid fertiliser at 1/3 strength. Should your plant be in flower from Autumn into Winter then continue feeding once a month.

Pruning & Grooming

The stems of Crown of Thorns break very easily, and the latex sap will drip out. To stop the latex dripping, spray the damaged area with water.

Grow More Plants

Crown of Thorns can be propagated by cutting tips about 10cm in length, with a sharp knife. Spray the cut areas with water to stop the sap leaking. Allow the cuttings to dry out for 24 hours and then plant in a mixture of half sand to half peat moss. Do not over-water.

ABUNDANCE
DESERT ROSE
Adenium obesum

Meanings
fertility, wealth, luck, prosperity, success, family

Uses
Invite Desert Rose into your home or working space to set a lasting foundation and encourage permanence of dreams, plans and values. Place near a front door or window to encourage prosperity and good luck. If you are having challenging family times, move to areas where the family come together in the evenings. Give to another to say, 'Good luck', 'I wish your family well' or 'Congratulations'.

CARE
houseplant maintenance level = easy

Profile
Desert Rose is a succulent known in China as 'Wealth Plant'. This curious-looking houseplant has a green-grey cone-shaped caudex (swollen base stem), from which a branching dark green stem grows. Leaves form on the ends of these branches and are joined by bright flowers, often in reds and pinks. Native to Arabia and eastern Africa, its appearance makes it popular as a 'false bonsai' due to the similarities with real specimens. Care needs to be taken when handling it because the sap is poisonous and irritating to the skin. This sap is used throughout Africa as an arrow poison for fish and game hunting. Highly toxic to humans and animals if ingested.

Container & Soil
You will need a free-draining soil mix such as two parts premium potting mix to one part vermiculite or a cactus-specific mix. Re-pot a little higher in the soil each time to encourage the thickening of the base stem.

Position & Light

This houseplant will require a full-sun position, but not the full midday sun. It does well on patios and in spots by windows.

Water

Water needs to be monitored closely. Never over-water or allow plant pot to sit in water. Although you can allow the top quarter depth of the soil to become a little dry at times, never let it dry out during the warmer months. Avoid watering the leaves and stems.

Food

Use a liquid fertiliser at half strength, preferably a seaweed-based formula, once every two weeks throughout the year, but not during the coldest Winter months.

Pruning & Grooming

Damage can occur due to cold. If damage occurs, tips can be pruned with a sterilised knife, to encourage additional branching. This can also be done to prohibit unwanted growth. When cutting, use rubbing alcohol or wipes to sterilise the blade between each cut made. This is best done in late Winter.

Grow More Plants

Although Desert Rose can be grown from cuttings, much better results are found via their seeds. You will not always end up with the same colours as the parent plant, however. Remove from seed pods and plant in a seed-raising mix.

DEVIL'S IVY

Epipremnum aureum

Meanings
delay, bind, capture, obtain, prosperity

Uses
If you wish to stop something occurring, or delay its progress, then this plant may help you. It can grow just about anywhere and will deter attacks, stop illness and denegation. The plant is also an excellent air purifier, so coupled with its energetic properties it makes a very good place-of-business plant. Give to another to say, 'I wish you success', 'Be patient' or 'I desire you'.

CARE
houseplant maintenance level = easy

Profile
A Polynesian native, this almost indestructible climbing vine, with beautiful heart-shaped glossy green and yellow or white marbled leaves, grows up to 20m in the wild but can be contained by pruning, if required. They will usually grow to about 1.5m (6ft) when grown indoors. Highly toxic to humans and animals if ingested.

Container & Soil
Plant in a container that is just a little bigger than the root ball if you want to contain growth. If not, select a size bigger. Use a good-quality indoor soil-based potting mix.

Position & Light
Find a place with filtered light to slight shade and average humidity.

Water
Have soil just damp throughout the Winter months. From early Spring to mid-Autumn (fall), let the soil just dry out between watering.

Food

Once every six months, feed with a slow-release complete fertiliser and then throughout Summer add to this a liquid fertiliser at full strength once every two weeks.

Pruning & Grooming

To create a bushy appearance and to contain growth, prune back new tips. These can also be used as cuttings to create new plants. Replace the top 4cm (2") of soil each Spring and re-pot and replace the soil every two years.

Grow More Plants

Take cuttings throughout Spring, from immediately below a node. Remove the bottom leaves and then plant in a mixture of half perlite and coarse sand and half damp peat moss or a commercial seed- and cutting-raising medium. Cover with plastic or a dome and place in bright filtered light. Expect the cutting to form roots in about six weeks when you may then re-pot.

OPPORTUNITY

ELEPHANT EAR

Alocasia x amazonica

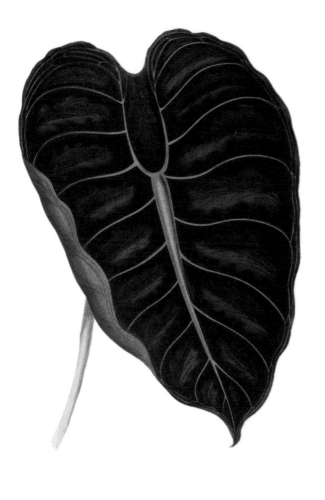

Meanings
freedom, fortune, rebirth, destiny, growth

Uses
Invite the Elephant Ear plant into areas where change is needed or happening, to encourage things to go in your favour. This plant is very good for new homes, businesses or workspaces or for those who are contemplating or taking steps towards new beginnings. It will help those in its environment to seek improvement and see and take advantage of opportunities quickly. Give to another to say, 'Good luck', 'It is time to begin again' or 'You are free'.

CARE
houseplant maintenance level = challenging

Profile
This plant's leaves are a stunning deepest dark-green huge elephant-ear shape veined and edged in white. It is just one of the Elephant Ear family and is also sometimes known as 'Amazonian Elephant Ear'. It is a popular hybrid that does not grow wild, but originated in Asia. The leaves can grow up to 60cm (24") in length and become 30cm (12") wide. The overall plant usually grows to 1.2m x 1m (4ft x 3ft) indoors with care. All parts are poisonous. Highly toxic to humans and animals if ingested.

Container & Soil
Use a potting mix of half soil-based compost and half composted bark for best results. Container needs to be roomy around the root ball.

Position & Light
Elephant Ear prefers a warm position with indirect light. Full light will cause damage. Humidity needs to be high.

Water

Care must be taken not to allow the plant to become waterlogged, but the soil must be kept moist over Summer. Allow the top of soil to slightly dry out between watering over the colder months. It is best to use rainwater or distilled water.

Food

Once every six months feed with a slow-release fertiliser and then from early Spring to mid-Summer add a liquid fertiliser once every two weeks.

Pruning & Grooming

Mist daily to increase humidity This plant will go into dormancy over Winter, however, so expect it to die back to the bulb, then.

Grow More Plants

In early Spring through to early Summer, small tubers can be removed from the root tips. These should be placed in damp vermiculite, covered with plastic and placed in a warm position in filtered light. Once established, re-pot as a mature plant.

CONNECTION

ENGLISH IVY

Hedera helix

Meanings
fidelity, fertility, protection, tenacity, immortality

Uses
English Ivy is a brilliant air purifier so is beneficial in this capacity anywhere you wish to place it. Due to its ability to connect people, ideas, community and plans, it works very well in living, dining and kitchen areas of the home, or places of work and commercial areas where people need to all get along together. English Ivy helps people stick at things, so it can be positioned in gyms and places where long-term projects are undertaken. Give to another to say, 'Don't give up', 'I am true to you' or 'I am always with you'.

CARE
houseplant maintenance level = easy

Profile
Leaves are leathery, have three to five deep lobes and the plant branches, so makes for a bushier type of ivy. It is a fast grower and produces nodes on the stems from which aerial roots will form. These roots will attach to damp surfaces and help the plant spread. It is native to Europe and parts of west Asia. In the wild it can attain a height of 20–30m (66–100ft) as it grows up trees and cliffs. Moderately toxic to dogs, cats and humans if ingested.

Container & Soil
Plant in a container with a support, or against a structure that the English Ivy can grow upon. Can also be potted in hanging baskets. Use a medium- to good-quality potting mix and top-dress each year.

Position & Light
Does fairly well in dim-lit areas, but will prefer bright filtered light and moderate humidity. Care needs to be taken not to place in areas with wide variations in temperature throughout the day and night.

Water

During the cooler months, allow the top few centimetres (about an inch) to dry out between watering. During the rest of the year, ensure that the soil stays just moist.

Food

Do not feed during the Winter months but feeding once a month all other times, with a full-strength liquid fertiliser, will help promote strong and healthy growth.

Pruning & Grooming

As your ivy grows, it will need support of some kind in the form of a trellis, stakes, pole or an object to cling to. Tie trailing ends to your support to help them anchor.

Grow More Plants

Cut a tip between 8–10cm (3–4") in length, from just above a growth bud, and then place in distilled or rain water in a clear jar. Put this in a bright and warm place and it should form roots within weeks. Pot a few cuttings together in one pot as described above.

FIDDLE-LEAF FIG

Ficus lyrata

Meanings

balance, understanding, relationships, partnerships, quiet

Uses

It is often thought that the Fiddle-leaf Fig is useful in office and commercial environments due to its larger architectural look. While this is true, it can also help bring a more harmonious and friendly energy to workplaces. Placed in family areas of the home – kitchens, living rooms and family rooms – it will help those within feel calm and connected. Give to another to say, 'You are welcome here', 'I agree with you' or 'I want to be with you'.

CARE

houseplant maintenance level = medium to challenging

Profile

In its natural habitat as an understory rainforest plant, it is usually very fast growing, and, depending on your indoor haven, you may enjoy similar results. This Ficus gets its name due to its large, fiddle-shaped leaves, which have been known to grow up to 4m (157") in height with leaves around 20cm (almost 9") in width. A native of western Africa, the plant usually begins its life as an epiphyte before anchoring itself in the soil and often becoming a large tree that grows 12 –15m (39—49ft) in height. Highly toxic to humans and animals if ingested and the sap is a skin irritant to all.

Container & Soil

Your plant will need to be re-potted each year in completely fresh potting mix. Containers need to allow for plenty of room for the roots and their fast growth.

Position & Light
The Fiddle-leaf enjoys a semi-bright position, good airflow, warmth and humidity. These make ideal living-area plants and must capture a few hours of direct morning light per day.

Water
Soil should be allowed to dry out between each watering, completely in Summer and just barely in the middle-Winter period. Generally, water lightly once every two weeks. Never mist.

Food
Feed every four weeks with a diluted-to-half-strength indoor plant-specific liquid fertiliser. You may find the addition of a slow release indoor plant food a couple of times a year is also helpful.

Pruning & Grooming
Fiddle-leaf Fig grows on a single stem, but you can prune the growth tip to encourage the formation of a divided stem. These plants are deemed 'difficult' because they are highly sensitive to chemicals. Re-potting with fresh soil every year and wiping leaves with a lightly damp cloth regularly will help.

Grow More Plants
In Spring, cut a fresh and healthy tip with one or two leaves. Place the stem in a glass of distilled water and place in a warm and sunny spot. Change water as it discolours. After roots appear (about a month), pot into a rich, moist mix.

FLAMING KATY

Kalanchoe blossfeldiana

Meanings

grounding, resilience, advancement, reinforcement, stability

Uses

Flaming Katy works well in areas where people meet and a harmonious, safe environment is required. Other ideal spaces are places of healing, areas of mental and emotional work, and living spaces that can be busy. Use in workspaces where there has been hostility, and the Flaming Katy will give strength and grounding and help everyone to move forward. Give to another to say, 'I wish you strength', 'You are safe here' or 'I am your friend'.

CARE

houseplant maintenance level = easy

Profile

Brilliant small bunches of flowers in reds, oranges, yellows and whites bounce up above the foliage throughout Spring and Summer and will last for around three months. These flowers make them a very cheerful indoor plant. Madagascar is where these plants are from, originally, and they will generally grow to be about 45 x 30cm (18 x 12"). Their foliage consists of leaves that are fleshy in texture. Non-toxic to humans, mildly toxic to dogs and cats.

Container & Soil

A commercial cactus-specific compost or a mixture of half good-quality indoor potting compost to half horticulture grit is the best medium in which to grow Flaming Katy.

Position & Light

Place the Flaming Katy in filtered sunlight, but it will also tolerate direct sun for part of the day. Humidity needs to be low.

Water

In the warmer seasons, this plant is best watered from the bottom of the container, by filling a tray or saucer that the pot stands in. Do so when soil becomes dry. Never let leaves become wet, as they may rot. In Winter, allow the soil to become dry between watering.

Food

From early Spring to late Summer feed once every two weeks with a liquid fertiliser at half strength.

Pruning & Grooming

Re-pot each Spring, replace soil mixture and go up one size in container. Cut out flowering stems once spent.

Grow More Plants

Take tip cuttings in Spring and plant in a commercial seed- and cutting-raising medium or a mixture of half damp peat moss and half coarse sand. Place in a warm position with filtered bright light and water as needed, but do not allow to become waterlogged.

FLAMING SWORD

Vriesea splendens

Meanings
truth, affirmation, intuition, detoxification, defence

Uses
The Flaming Sword will bring heightened mental and intellectual energies to the spaces you choose to place it in. Invite it in to share your workspace, to inspire confidence and heighten intuition. Those who practise counselling, metaphysical modalities and who teach will also find that this plant creates a very conducive environment for these professions. Give to another to say, 'You can do this', 'I believe in you' or 'I will protect you'.

CARE
houseplant maintenance level = average

Profile
Thick deep-green strap-like leaves are patterned with rusty brown horizontal stripes. The leaves grow to create a well in the middle of the Flaming Sword bromeliad. The common name comes from the brilliant red sword of the flower structure, which can grow to 60cm (24") in length and consists of tight scarlet bracts that hold, within them, tiny sunny-yellow flowers. Overall, this plant – native to Trinidad, the Guianas and Venezuela – usually grows to 60 x 45cm (24 x 18"). Non-toxic to humans and animals.

Container & Soil
Lives best in a container slightly bigger than the plant. Use a commercial bromeliad potting mix or a medium of half commercial orchid mix to half good-quality indoor potting compost. Ensure that whatever you use is only packed lightly.

Position & Light
This plant needs filtered light and moderate humidity level.

Water

Leaves form a centre well and this should be filled with rainwater or distilled water and kept topped up as needed. Water the soil when it feels dry and also mist with water a few times a week.

Food

Best feed with a foliar liquid fertiliser at ¼ the recommended strength and spray the leaves with it once a month between early Spring until mid-Autumn (fall).

Pruning & Grooming

Re-pot in Spring in a one-size-larger container. Remove flower spike once spent.

Grow More Plants

Offsets will form around the time flowering occurs. Separate from the main plant with a sharp knife, ensuring that you have left roots attached, when they are at least 8cm in length. Pot in same mixture as mature plants, but cover in plastic for about six weeks until established, and then re-pot.

GROWTH

FRUIT SALAD PLANT

Monstera deliciosa

Meanings
opportunity, expansion, honour, action, plans

Uses
The Fruit Salad Plant works well in spaces where new ventures are being planned or created. For this reason they work very well in offices, artistic spaces and are a good choice in a new home, especially those undergoing renovations. If you are having trouble making plans, creating goals, lists, or making decisions, sit by one of these plants to help you see potential more clearly. Give to another to say, 'Good luck', 'I respect your efforts' or as a housewarming present to say, 'Congratulations and I wish you well'.

CARE
houseplant maintenance level = easy

Profile
This popular houseplant's leaves bounce out with their heart-shaped dark emerald faces, which indicate (so well!) their meanings. Fruit Salad Plant is also known as 'Swiss Cheese Plant' or by its Latin name 'Monstera', and is an easy-care beginner houseplant. Originally from southern Mexico, they can attain a height in excess of 9m (30ft). This plant's fruit is edible and said to be a combination in scent and taste of pineapple and banana, but all the rest of this plant is mildly toxic, so you need to be careful with its placement around children and pets.

Container & Soil
The perfect potting mix for this plant is about 1/3 sand to 2/3 good potting soil. Add a layer of about 4cm (1.5") of compost in early Spring and re-pot when the plant begins to crowd the pot, but at least every three years.

Position & Light

Fruit Salad Plant likes a warm place to live, and although you will find that Fruit Salad Plant can grow in darker areas, it will be healthier in strong, filtered light.

Water

During Winter, you can let the soil just dry out between watering. Ensure that the soil stays moist throughout the warmer Spring and Summer months.

Food

From the warmer Spring months until mid-Autumn (fall), feeding once a month with a liquid fertiliser specifically for indoor plants, at full strength, will ensure healthy growth.

Pruning & Grooming

If you are looking at keeping your plant small, prune back in Spring to the shape and size you desire. Leaves need to be wiped over with a damp cloth regularly to remove dust and indoor chemicals.

Grow More Plants

There are many ways to propagate this plant, but taking cuttings is a rather easy option. To do so, remove a stem just below a leaf node and prune off any lower leaves. Place the stem directly into a pot or in a glass of distilled water and wait until roots appear.

GOLDEN CANE PALM

Dypsis lutescens

Meanings

alignment, strength, abundance, reward, success

Uses

From a health point of view, Golden Cane Palm is almost essential in bedrooms because it cleanses the air, produces oxygen and is a natural humidifier. It can also help those within the room find alignment during sleep. Place at the front of homes and businesses to encourage success, and in the workplace to encourage promotion and strength. Give to another to say, 'Congratulations', 'I wish you success', 'I understand you'.

CARE

houseplant maintenance level = easy

Profile

Arching golden-green feathery fronds can grow to 60cm (24") in length indoors, which is why it has also earned the common names 'Butterfly Palm' and 'Golden Feather Palm'. But it is also known as 'Areca Palm'. The plant can grow 6–12m (20–39ft) in height outdoors in the right conditions. It is native to Madagascar, the Philippines and southern India. Non-toxic to humans and animals.

Container & Soil

This palm will grow to suit its pot, so select a container that suits the size you wish your plant to grow to. Stand pot on a tray or saucer of wet pebbles, to increase humidity, if required, especially in Summer.

Position & Light

A spot with filtered sunlight is best. Humidity levels should be moderate.

Water

Golden Cane Palm needs to be watered well in the warmer months. Keep the soil damp. Watering can be reduced during Winter when you can allow the top to dry slightly between waterings.

Food

Feed Golden Cane Palm every two weeks from early Spring through to mid-Summer, with a liquid fertiliser.

Pruning & Grooming

Re-potting only needs to be undertaken every five to ten years or when you wish the palm top to grow larger. Do this in Spring and replace soil when you do.

Grow More Plants

Remove suckers of at least 30cm (12") in Spring, ensuring that some roots are retained. Plant into a pot of 1/3 perlite or coarse sand and 2/3 soil-based potting mix. Water soil and then cover with plastic and place in a warm place with filtered light for about six weeks until established. Re-pot once suckers have taken root.

HAWORTHIA

Haworthia spp.

Meanings
deflection, prevention, reversal, clearing, awareness

Uses
In some South African villages, Haworthia is placed around the outsides of homes to protect against witchcraft attacks. Placing on a windowsill or at a front or back door will help shield those within from all types of negative and malevolent attacks. This plant also reverses bad luck and negativity, and clears away unwanted energies. Haworthia is helpful near work spaces to protect projects and space, and will lift your awareness.

CARE
houseplant maintenance level = easy

Profile
The Haworthia is a small South African succulent, popular for its distinctive spiked-shaped stems that are often textured and coloured with delightful patterns. There are over 80 species, but most are approximately 20 x 15cm (8 x 6") in dimension and grow long tubular white flowers on a slender stem, in Summer. Non-toxic to humans and animals.

Container & Soil
Grow in containers that are only just larger than your plant, or in groupings within a larger pot. Use a cactus/succulent-specific potting mix, or you can make your own by mixing 2/3 good quality indoor potting mix to 1/3 perlite or coarse sand.

Position & Light
A bright, sunny spot (but not too hot), is the right place for this plant. They will tolerate semi-shade very well, too, but they need good airflow at all times.

Water

Watering needs to be carefully undertaken. Throughout the colder Winter months, allow to just dry out. Let the top of the soil dry out between watering from early Spring through to mid-Autumn (fall).

Food

Feeding is optional, as they really should not require it, but if the plant is growing poorly, then feed with a liquid fertiliser at 1/3 strength once a month from early Spring through to mid-Autumn.

Pruning & Grooming

The plant only needs to be re-potted when it outgrows its container. Do this in Spring and completely replace the potting mix when you do.

Grow More Plants

Offsets are usually found during the Summer and these can be gently pulled off the main plant. Offsets with roots can simply be re-potted as described above. Those without roots must be left to dry for three days in a shaded, airy place, and then planted as described above.

HEART LEAF

Philodendron hederaceum

Meanings
happiness, passion, growth, devotion, appreciation

Uses
Heart Leaf can be placed in areas where couples spend their time, to inspire and encourage romance, and deepen love. In work areas it will help people find their passion and enable them to view co-workers with appreciation and kindness. No matter where Heart Leaf lives, it will help grow ideas, feelings, happiness and positivity. Give to another to say, 'Thank you', 'I love you' or 'I am happy for you'.

CARE
houseplant maintenance level = easy

Profile
Emerald-coloured heart-shaped leaves tumble gently from this fast-growing Central American climber. Leaves are a beautiful bronze when young and then slowly become a deep green as they mature. The plant can attain a length of 1.5m (5ft) and the trails can be trained around a pole to create a full-shaped plant, or left to climb or trail, so care must be taken around pets and children.

Container & Soil
Can be grown in a large pot containing a pole, stake or trellis for this plant to grow upon, or, when young, can be grown in a hanging basket. Use a mix of 2/3 good-quality indoor potting mix to 1/3 perlite or coarse sand.

Position & Light
The Heart Leaf requires a position that has filtered sunlight, but it will also tolerate light shade. The plant grows best with humidity that is low to average.

Water

Throughout Spring and Summer the plant will enjoy light misting. From mid-Spring to mid-Autumn (fall) ensure that the soil stays damp. In the colder Winter months only water when the top of the soil is dry.

Food

From Spring to mid-Summer feed with a liquid fertiliser once every two weeks.

Pruning & Grooming

Re-pot when the plant outgrows its container. This is best done in Spring. If not required, replace the top 4cm (2") of soil. Prune in late Winter and pinch out new growth tips any time as they appear to encourage more compact growth. Wipe leaves each month with a damp cloth.

Grow More Plants

From late Spring through to early Summer cuttings can be taken to propagate. Cut these just below a node and ensure they are 8–10cm long (3–4"). Remove lower leaves and plant in a mixture of half peat moss to half pearlite of coarse sand or a commercial seed- and cutting-raising mix. Place in a warm, humid position and cover with a plastic dome. Roots should appear in a month and can be removed and re-potted.

HENS AND CHICKS

Sempervivum tectorum

Meanings

eternity, purification, calmness, clarity, protection

Uses

Grow on the roof or place on a high shelf across from a window to protect against attacks and lightning strikes. It really does need full sun to grow well, so find the sunniest places in which you work, study and live where you require greater clarity, protection and longevity in your projects. Hens and Chicks will help those who are unwell, by providing purification, protection and the energies of survival. Give to another to say, 'I am with you forever', 'I wish you peace' or 'I believe you can do this'.

CARE

houseplant maintenance level = easy

Profile

A beautiful green rosette of leaves form the Hens and Chicks plant. Also known as 'Houseleek', it is an Alpine succulent that is super easy to care for. They can grow up to 30cm (12") in diameter and can form a mat of plants as they send out runners from which more plants grow. When flowers appear, they are tiny star-shaped bells, which herald the death of the plant but not the so-called 'Chicks' it offsets. Non-toxic to humans and animals.

Container & Soil

Grow in a container only slightly larger than the plant and use a medium of 1/3 coarse sand and 2/3 soil-based compost or a commercial cactus/succulent mix.

Position & Light

Place in a position that receives full sun, but this plant will also tolerate filtered bright light for part of the day. Humidity needs are low.

Water

The Hens and Chicks plant requires sparse watering. From early Spring through to late Summer, only water when the top of the soil dries out. Through the colder months only water once a month.

Food

From early Spring to late Autumn (fall) feed once a month with a liquid fertiliser made up to half the regular strength.

Pruning & Grooming

Only needs re-potting when plant becomes root-bound in container. Re-pot and replace soil in Spring. After the plant flowers, the leaves will die and new plants will appear. Remove the flower when spent and ensure that 'Chicks' are also removed, to prevent overcrowding.

Grow More Plants

Propagation can be achieved through division by gently removing the 'Chicks' growing on the edges of the mature plant. These can simply be replanted as a mature plant.

LUCK

JADE PLANT

Crassula ovata

Meanings
abundance, finances, contentment, accomplishment, independence

Uses
In the Asian practice of Feng Shui, the Jade Plant is traditionally placed in the south-eastern corner of a room or home, where it can help increase wealth. In Western folklore, placing a plant near a front door encourages abundance, luck and good fortune, and touching the plant as you pass it will boost good luck. The Jade Plant does very well near windows that receive a few hours of sunlight a day. They are found in many places of trading and business.

CARE
houseplant maintenance level = easy

Profile
This divine succulent's leaves are a lovely deep forest green. Their shape is an ovaldisc of about 2–3cm (just over an inch) in width. Each leaf is edged in deep crimson and they grow from branches that are gnarled and textured, resembling a miniature old oak. Interestingly, this plant originates from Africa and is a very popular houseplant across the world due to it being an evergreen and easy to grow. It is said that you need to kill one three times before it actually dies. Moderately toxic to humans and highly toxic to animals if ingested.

Container & Soil
A pot that is only slightly bigger than your plant is best. Go only slightly up in size when re-potting into a new container. A soil mix can be created from two parts good-quality indoor potting mix to one-part coarse sand or perlite.

Position & Light

Jade Plant prefers low humidity and can survive in filtered light, but prefers somewhere between this and a bright light. Although cultivars rarely flower, no Jade Plant will blossom without a few hours of direct sunlight a day.

Water

For most of the year, water very lightly, letting the soil stay rather dry. During the warmest Summer period, you will need to increase the watering frequency, but they really do best being dry.

Food

A light dose of a yearly or half-yearly slow-release fertiliser is all that is required. Overfeeding can be detrimental.

Pruning & Grooming

Re-pot every three years and replace the potting mix when you do. Although you can prune this plant to reshape it, if desired, it really is not necessary because they naturally grow to a lovely tree shape on their own.

Grow More Plants

Take a cutting from a new growth area or an offset in Spring, or, even easier, remove individual leaves. Plant any of these into a mixture of 50 per cent sand and 50 per cent peat moss. Once established, re-pot into potting mix as recommended above. Keep in a warm position in bright indirect light.

MAIDENHAIR FERN

Adiantum raddianum

Meanings
protection, expression, purpose, self-knowledge, sensitivity

Uses
Use in places where you are undertaking study or anywhere in the home, to ease your mind when emotional trauma and upsets have been hard to overcome. The Maidenhair Fern is very helpful on meeting-room tables, in classrooms and on reception desks because it allows all those present to express themselves fully and to be sensitive to others. Give to another to say, 'I am sorry', 'I wish you well with your studies' or 'I wish you safety'.

CARE
houseplant maintenance level = challenging

Profile
Fine and light delicate forest-green triangular leaves seem to dance upon the arching black stems of the beautiful, and a little fussy, Maidenhair Fern. Observing the plant in person one can see the similarity to human hair, hence the reason for its common name. Also known as the 'Delta Maidenhair Fern', it is a native of Brazil and Venezuela and grows to a size of about 50 x 80cm (20 x 32") as an indoor plant. Non-toxic to humans and animals.

Container & Soil
Use a container that gives the root ball a bit of space. Use a good-quality soil-based indoor potting mix. Stand the container on a tray or saucer of wet pebbles.

Position & Light
Maidenhair Fern will need a place with filtered sunlight or light shade. It will require a humid environment. Ensure that the plant is kept away from draughts.

Water

This plant needs to be kept moist at all times, throughout all seasons, although you can reduce watering a little in Winter. You can sometimes revive this plant successfully if it dries out by submerging the pot in water until the soil is fully wet.

Food

It does well with a slow-release fertiliser once every six months, and from mid-Spring through to the end of Summer add a liquid fertiliser once every two weeks.

Pruning & Grooming

In early Spring, cut back hard to the base any growth that is brown or unsightly. Pruning like this will encourage fresh, new growth. Re-pot every two years in the Spring and replace the potting medium as you do.

Grow More Plants

When re-potting, the Maidenhair Fern can simply be divided into new clumps and replanted. At this time, small sections of the rhizome, with roots attached, can also be pulled off and replanted.

PROSPERITY

MONEY TREE

Pachira aquatica

Meanings
happiness, money, abundance, success, luck

Uses
The Money Tree is traditionally placed in areas of business, to attract money and to bring luck. The stems of this plant are sometimes plaited, and red ribbons are often added to boost the luck and powers of this plant. To grow this plant and keep it in good health will, it is said, bring you ultimate happiness and money. Give to another to say, 'Good luck', 'I hope you prosper' or 'May you find happiness'.

CARE
houseplant maintenance level = moderate

Profile
Large glossy emerald-green lobed leaf arrangements form the foliage of this plant, which is native to the Central and South American swamps. As a houseplant, they usually grow to about 1.2m (6ft), but in the wild they have been known to attain a height of 18m (59ft). They rarely, if at all, flower as a houseplant, which is a shame because their flowers are one of the largest and most unusual tree flowers in the world. Yellow-cream flower buds are 35.5cm (14") in length and open to clusters of long, cream-coloured stamens tipped in red. Non-toxic to humans and animals.

Container & Soil
Money Trees are rather fast growing, but you can contain them a little longer and even train to become a bonsai, by selecting a pot that will just fit your plant and by pruning growth tips. Soil needs to be very free-draining, so it is recommended to use ¾ light potting mix to ¼ course sand.

Position & Light

The Money Tree likes filtered sunlight and moderate humidity. They do not fare well in direct sunlight.

Water

Even though this swamp plant loves moisture, care must still be taken not to over-water. Have the soil slightly wet through the cold months and then for the rest of the year only water when the top of the soil is dry. Increase humidity by standing the pot on a tray of wet pebbles, but do not let tray become full of water.

Food

From the beginning of Spring until mid-Autumn (fall) feed with a liquid fertiliser at half strength once every two weeks.

Pruning & Grooming

If you would like to retain a more compact and bushy shape, pinch off the growth tips. Replace the top third of the soil each year in late Autumn and re-pot when the plant becomes root-bound only.

Grow More Plants

To propagate, take a cutting between late Spring and mid-Summer, from a growth tip, and plant directly into a small pot in a soil base recommended above.

COMMUNICATION

MOTH ORCHID

Phalaenopsis spp.

Meanings
compassion, shield, consciousness, peace, sensuality

Uses
Moth Orchids make good bedroom plants because they heighten sensuality, (as all orchids commonly do) and they inspire peace and provide support for all levels of consciousness. Another interesting benefit of the Moth Orchid is that it works as a shield for unwanted energy. It also facilitates communication, so is excellent on reception desks and service counters and in the entrances of homes or living areas. Give to another to say, 'I am thinking of you', 'Let's talk' or 'I wish you peace'.

CARE
houseplant maintenance level = easy

Profile
Gracefully arching long stems of orchid flowers rise above the foliage of the Moth Orchid. They are native to parts of Asia and South-East Asia, Australia and New Guinea. These flowers can blossom at any time of the year, last up to a month and, with care, can re-flower. The low-growing foliage base of large dark sage-green oval leaves still makes a lovely green houseplant even without the magnificent flowers. In the wild, this epiphyte grows up to 90cm (2ft) in height. Non-toxic to humans and animals.

Container & Soil
Moth Orchids are prone to root rot, so pot in a container that has holes so that water can completely drain. Do not grow in standard potting, compost or soil mixes; rather, a commercial orchid preparation or chipped bark is best.

Position & Light
This plant requires bright light, but it must be indirect. Harsh, full light will be detrimental. It enjoys moderate humidity.

Water

Moth Orchids will grow best if they are watered with the purest water you can find. This could be rainwater or distilled water. Do not overwater and allow the top of growing medium to dry out slightly between watering. Mist to raise humidity and ensure that aerial roots stay hydrated.

Food

Moth Orchids will need to be fed every two weeks with a liquid-based fertiliser.

Pruning & Grooming

To encourage new blooms, prune the spent flower just above the second band on the stem, from the bottom.

Grow More Plants

If shoots develop at the base of the plant, wait until roots begin to form and then carefully remove and re-pot. The new shoot will need a warmer environment, very little water and bright filtered conditions for the first six weeks until it has established.

PAINTED LEAVES

Plectranthus scutellarioides

Meanings
awakening, visions, memory, sleep, imagination

Uses
The Painted Leaves plant is one of the very best bedroom plants because it assists with dream recall and can provide a deep, more restful sleep. Placed in creative working spaces it also encourages imagination and awakens personal connections with projects. In work and study places, it can help with memory retention. Give to another to say, 'Sweet dreams', 'I honour our memories' or 'You inspire me'.

CARE
houseplant maintenance level = easy

Profile
A jewel-like assortment of leaf shapes and colours in lime green, hot pink, rusty orange and velvet burgundy make this a delightful houseplant. This hybrid is also known as 'Coleus' or 'Painted Nettle'. The original parent plants are from South-East Asia and Australia. They grow to about 60 x 30cm (24 x 12") in size and all parts are highly toxic to humans and animals if ingested or long periods of contact occur, so care must be taken around pets and children.

Container & Soil
Select a container big enough to fit the plant, with a little extra growth room. Growing medium should be half good-quality soil-based potting mix and half compost-based potting mix.

Position & Light
Prefers filtered bright sunlight and average humidity. A warm position is best.

Water

From mid-Spring through to the end of Autumn ensure that the soil is always kept moist, but then, in Winter, it is helpful to let the top of the soil dry out between waterings.

Food

Feed from the beginning of Spring until the end of Autumn (fall) with a liquid fertiliser, every two weeks.

Pruning & Grooming

Pinch out and discard stem tips as they appear to encourage better, thicker foliage growth. In late Winter, prune the plant back to 1/3 of its size.

Grow More Plants

Take tip cuttings that are at least 5cm in length and place in cutting-specific commercial raising mixture or a good-quality soil-based potting mix. Water, and place in a warm position. They should establish and take root in about 2–3 weeks. Re-pot as a mature plant.

PEACE LILY

Spathiphyllum wallisii

Meanings
dedication, cleansing, purification, healing, balance

Uses
NASA has proven that the Peace Lily reduces air pollution. It is also believed that they absorb radiation[1], so having them in areas where there are electronic devices or potential radiation, such as offices and workplaces, is a wonderful idea. They will also remove negativity, purify energy and offer peace, balance and healing. For this reason, they make perfect companions for those who are ill. Give to another to say, 'Get well soon', 'I wish you calm' or 'I believe in you'.

CARE
houseplant maintenance level = easy

Profile
Large glossy ribbed dark leaves are a beautiful feature of this plant, but so too is the long, graceful white spathe that rises above the foliage and forms a backdrop to the spike of tiny bright-yellow flowers. The Peace Lily plant comes from Central America with dimensions of up to 60 x 60cm (24 x 24"). The entire plant is poisonous, so care needs to be taken with its position. Highly toxic to humans and animals if ingested.

Container & Soil
The pot you decide on for the Peace Lily needs to accommodate the root system and the best soil is one created from half compost-based mix to half best-quality indoor potting soil.

---

[1]   *BC Wolverton; WL Douglas; K Bounds (September 1989). Interior landscape plants for indoor air pollution abatement (Report). NASA. NASA-TM-101766.*

Position & Light

The Peace Lily enjoys bright light, but it must be indirect. They do better in a slightly warm room, but not one that's overheated.

Water

Peace Lily needs a moist soil for most of the year, but during Winter it is better to allow the top few centimetres (about an inch) to dry out between watering.

Food

Twice a year, feed with a slow-release fertiliser and then, from mid-Spring to the end of Summer, feed with a liquid fertiliser at full strength once every two weeks.

Pruning & Grooming

Re-potting should only be done when you find your plant is root-bound, which would normally occur about every 1–2 years (depending on pot). Deadhead flower spikes once spent and remove dead and yellowed leaves as yellowing occurs.

Grow More Plants

Peace Lily plants can be divided. Do this during Spring by lifting from the soil and carefully pulling apart clumps to retain foliage and roots in each. The plant also produces smaller offsets, and these can be carefully separated from the main plant.

FAITH
PRAYER PLANT
Maranta leuconeura

Meanings
relaxation, meditation, peace, spirituality, hope

Uses
Prayer Plants thrive in a humid environment, so bathrooms are a favoured spot. You will find that they can make good bedroom, retreat and relaxation area additions, too, if you can maintain high humidity. This plant will assist you in keeping hope alive, instilling faith in others (of you) and bring calm and peace. Give to another to say, 'I believe in you', 'I hope all goes well' or to mark religious and spiritual initiations and celebrations.

CARE
houseplant maintenance level = easy

Profile
Each evening the leaves of this unusual plant come together as if in prayer and when dawn breaks, they release and open. The underside of each leaf is a deep red while the top is patterned in delicate dark and light greens with red veins. Prayer Plants are from Central and South America and the West Indies and grow to about 60 x 60cm (24 x 24 "). Non-toxic to humans and animals.

Container & Soil
The Prayer Plant grows best in a rich, commercial compost-based potting mix, or you can make one by mixing 2/3 good-quality indoor potting mix and 1/3 compost. Use shallow containers for this plant because they have a small root system.

Position & Light
This plant will do best in a humid environment with filtered sunlight. Be careful not to position it near draughts, especially cold ones. The plant will not survive in temperatures under 12C (54F).

Water

In the warmer months, make sure that the soil is always moist. Through Winter, let it dry a little between watering. Misting a few times a week will keep humidity high, as will standing the pot on a bed of wet pebbles.

Food

Between Spring and Autumn (fall), feed every two weeks with a liquid fertiliser; but only use at half the recommended strength. When first potting, or when re-potting, a yearly slow-release fertiliser is recommended.

Pruning & Grooming

Re-pot each year in mid-Spring, and replace the soil. Older leaves can be pruned, to improve the appearance of the plant. Brown leaves indicate that your plant needs more humidity.

Grow More Plants

Take cuttings by slicing healthy leaf stalks of two or three leaves. With a sharp knife, peel the outer surface of the stalk, and then plant in a seed- or cutting-raising potting mix.

QUEEN OF HEARTS

Homalomena spp.

Meanings

nurturing, affection, vulnerability, care, compassion

Uses

Queen of Hearts is a wonderful family room-, kitchen- and living-room plant. It empowers the sense of family and belonging, and care and safety that a home should provide. It is also wonderful for those healing from injury or illness, or, generally, in places of healing. Invite Queen of Hearts to sit on your desk or table when you want to embrace and celebrate your vulnerabilities. Give to another to say, 'I love you', 'I care' or 'I hear you'.

CARE

houseplant maintenance level = easy

Profile

Heart-shaped glossy green leaves sit upon slender long red petioles. Native to southern Asia, the south west Pacific and Latin America, some also have interesting patterns upon their leaves. Many Homalomena also have a strong scent of anise and it is interesting to note that they are a relative of the Philodendron and grow well together with this species. Some Queen of Hearts plants are mildly toxic if ingested by humans or animals.

Container & Soil

Use a container that gives the plant some room, and plant in a mixture of $2/3$ good-quality indoor potting mix to $1/3$ perlite or coarse sand.

Position & Light

Place in a warm position, where your Queen of Hearts can sit in bright but indirect light. Avoid direct sun as this will burn the plant.

Water

From mid-Spring through to late Summer the soil must be kept moist, but do not over-water.

Food

Every six months it is beneficial to feed with a slow-release fertiliser, specifically for indoor plants, and then supplement this from Spring through to the end of Summer with a liquid fertiliser once every two weeks.

Pruning & Grooming

There are no special pruning needs because the plant is very disease resistant.

Grow More Plants

Division is the easiest way to create new plants. In Spring, if re-potting, gently pull the clumps apart and replant in new pots.

RAINBOW PINCUSHION
Mammillaria rhodantha

Meanings
freedom, wholeness, meditation, consciousness, emotion

Uses
Rainbow Pincushion works well on the windowsills in rooms of those who are emotionally entangled in situations they need to work through. In bedrooms it works with the dream state, to calm the unconscious mind, and in kitchens and areas of exercise it will help those within focus on wholeness and health. Place near doorways when wanting freedom of some sort. Give to another to say, 'I care for you', 'I hope you find the answers you seek' or 'Fly and be free'.

CARE
houseplant maintenance level = easy

Profile
A crown of bright magenta flowers blossoms upon the Rainbow Pincushion, from Spring right through to the beginning of Autumn. For the rest of the year, the delightful round pincushion-shaped cactus still provides interesting texture in a houseplant collection. Covered completely in very sharp spikes, care will be needed when selecting placement. A native of Mexico, it can grow to 15 x 30cm (6 x 8") in size. Non-toxic to humans and animals.

Container & Soil
Select a container only slightly larger than the plant. A medium of $1/5$ perlite, $1/5$ coarse sand and $3/5$ soil-based compost or a commercial cactus potting mix must be used.

Position & Light
Place in a spot in filtered sun through the hotter Summer months, and then reposition to capture direct sun for the rest of the year. They do not do well in artificial heating and require low humidity.

Water

From early Spring to late Autumn, water only when the top 2cm (3/4") is allowed to dry out. In Winter, only water once or twice.

Food

From mid-Spring until late Summer, feed with a cactus-specific fertiliser once a month.

Pruning & Grooming

Re-pot in Spring every 1–2 years, and replace soil when you do.

Grow More Plants

Offsets appear around the base and these can be carefully removed with a sharp knife while wearing heavy-duty gloves. Leave for a few days to dry and and then replant as described above

RUBBER PLANT

Ficus elastica

Meanings
study, restoration, action, exuberance, interest

Uses
Rubber Plant is an excellent air purifier, removing chemicals from the air, and even eliminating mould spores and bacteria. It also helps people stay focused, aids concentration and develops deeper interest in work that must be done. For this reason, it makes a wonderful plant for places of study, work, restoration (personal and physical) and creativity. The Rubber Plant moves thoughts into action and keeps spirits up. Give to another to say, 'I wish you well with your studies', 'Don't give up' or 'I hope you feel better soon'.

CARE
houseplant maintenance level = easy

Profile
When grown indoors, this south and south-east Asian plant's glossy dark large, leathery leaves form what appears to be a small tree. In the wild, the Rubber Plant can grow up to 30m (98ft), but will usually only attain a height of 1.8m (6ft) indoors. Some types feature lighter variegated leaves, which makes for an interesting display in a collection of Rubber Plants. These plants usually need more sunlight than their dark-leaf-coloured cousins. Mildly toxic to humans and moderately toxic to animals if ingested, plus the sap is a skin irritant, so care must be taken with positioning them and when pruning.

Container & Soil
A close-fitting pot is best and use a good-quality soil-based indoor potting mixture.

Position & Light

Never place Rubber Plant in direct sunlight. The leaves will burn. Instead, it enjoys filtered, indirect light. They do not tolerate large fluctuations in temperature, or draughts.

Water

Throughout the Winter months, ensure that the soil stays damp but not waterlogged. From mid-Spring until late Summer, water when the top of the soil has dried.

Food

The Rubber Plant grows well in a commercial slow-release fertiliser specifically for indoor plants. This can be supplemented with a liquid fertiliser every month from mid-Spring to late Summer.

Pruning & Grooming

Re-pot every 2–3 years, but only when roots begin to appear in drainage holes. Wait till Spring to do this, and completely replace the potting mix. Also prune in Spring to encourage a more busy and compact appearance. Mist with cool water every few days in the hotter summer months. If the plant is oozing sap, sprinkle the cut or break where the sap is present, with powdered charcoal.

Grow More Plants

Take a tip cutting of about 15cm in length just below a node. Remove lower leaf or leaves and plant into a commercial propagating mix or a mixture of ½ moist peat moss to ½ perlite or coarse sand. Cover with a plastic dome and place in filtered bright light in a warm position. Water only if it looks dry, which is unlikely. When new growth occurs, re-pot.

FLEXIBILITY

SNAKE PLANT

Sansevieria trifasciata

Meanings
creativity, technology, truth, healing, strength

Uses
Snake Plant is one of the best natural air purifiers, so is beneficial for those with respiratory issues. Place the Snake Plant in bedrooms and they will clear the air and induce healing, renewed strength and creative inspiration during sleep. Use near computers and other electronic devices to ensure positive energy and protection, and in areas people meet to encourage diplomacy and flexibility. Give to others to say, 'We can work this out', 'I believe you in you' or 'Get well'.

CARE
houseplant maintenance level = easy

Profile
Silver-marbled deep-green leaves stand straight in close clumps to form this plant from West Africa. Overall, the plant usually grows to be about 30 x 75cm (12 x 30"). All parts are toxic, so care must be taken not to have this plant near pets and children. Snake Plant is also known as 'Mother-in-law's Tongue' or 'Devil's Tongue', and is known for being almost indestructible. Toxic to humans, moderately toxic to dogs, mildly toxic to cats if ingested.

Container & Soil
Although they are very hardy, Snake Plants need very good drainage. Place drainage medium (stones or broken pots) in the bottom of a container with plenty of drainage holes. Plant in a mixture of $2/3$ good-quality potting mix and $1/3$ coarse sand. The container only needs to be slightly bigger than the plant.

Position & Light

Find an area with low humidity. When it comes to light, you will find that Snake Plant can tolerate both very dim areas and bright filtered light.

Water

Generally water once every two weeks from mid-Spring to mid-Autumn (fall) and then through the colder months, only once a month. Always let the top of the soil dry out.

Food

From mid-Spring through to mid-Autumn (fall), feed with a liquid fertiliser made up at half recommended strength, once every two weeks

Pruning & Grooming

Re-potting won't need to be undertaken more than once every few years. Remove all the old soil and replenish with a fresh mixture and do not go up too big in pot size. The Snake Plant is prone to rot from overwatering. Remove any damaged leaves as needed by cutting close to bottom.

Grow More Plants

Snake Plant can be propagated by division. Once plant is very established, remove, shake off soil and pull apart into smaller sections. Replant in containers and soil as suggested above.

SPIDER PLANT

Chlorophytum comosum

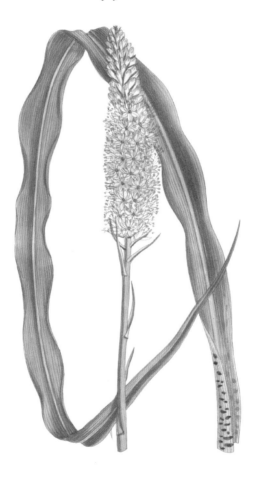

Meanings

mindfulness, protection, creativity, healing, independence

Uses

Spider Plant is a very good air cleaner and with its qualities of promoting healing, mindfulness and offering protection, it would make a good bedroom plant, too. Invite into creative spaces, meditation and study areas, and it will help you keep to your plans, especially if placed near front doors. Give to another to say, 'I know you can do this', 'You are doing well', 'I wish you a safe journey'.

CARE

houseplant maintenance level = easy

Profile

From a fountain-like clump of long, thin apple-green and cream striped leaves, baby plantlets spring forth and swing from long stems below. In the wilds of South Africa, where it originates, Spider Plant would send out these plantlets to form new plants in the earth surrounding it. Spider Plant grows to be about 12 x 60cm (91 x 2ft). Non-toxic to humans, dogs and most animals; mildly toxic to cats if ingested.

Container & Soil

Plant up in a pot or a hanging basket that will fit the root ball with a little extra room. Use a mixture of half compost-based potting mix and half regular potting mix.

Position & Light

Find a position that enjoys filtered sunlight, but this plant will also tolerate light shade. Humidity needs are low.

Water

Spider Plants are generally drought tolerant. You will need to water them from early Spring to the mid-Autumn (fall) when the top of the soil feels dry. During the colder months, the soil can dry out between watering. They are sensitive to fluoride, which will show up as spots upon the leaves. Unfortunately fluoride damage is irreversible, but you can try to avoid by watering with distilled water.

Food

Between mid-Spring through to early Autumn, Spider Plant will benefit from an application of a liquid fertiliser once every two weeks.

Pruning & Grooming

When the plant becomes root-bound, re-pot (preferably in Spring). This will usually be every two years. Replace the soil when you re-pot.

Grow More Plants

Plantlets can be simply cut from the plant and potted.

SPLIT ROCK

Pleiospilos nelii

Meanings
separateness, endurance, obstacles, positivity, mending

Uses
Split Rock can be used in areas where meditation is undertaken, so that everyone can retain their autonomy and power but still work together on a common goal. Place in homes that are undergoing renovations, have on tables and desks when people are working on challenging issues and projects, and invite into places where people are recovering from an accident or illness. Give to another to say, 'Get well soon', 'I am trying to understand' or 'We can overcome this'.

CARE
houseplant maintenance level = challenging

Profile
Looking exactly as the name suggests, a little rock that has a split in it, this succulent is simply a pair of leaves. From within its 'split', another pair will form and push out to feed off the old and eventually replace them. And so the cycle will continue. This South African native is found in lovely sage greens and soft purples and, when and if, they do bloom they will form large bright flowers that open in the afternoon and shut at dusk. Non-toxic to humans and animals.

Container & Soil
Select a small, though deep, container – this plant has a long tap root. Use a succulent/cactus commercial mix – do not use soil or compost. When planting, do not water for a few weeks and roots will be encouraged to establish.

Position & Light
Throughout much of the year the Split Rock will require full sun in a warm position. In the Summer months, however, they are better in a bright spot with filtered light. Humidity needs to be very low.

Water

Only water when the soil dries out completely and do not water at all during the peaks of Summer and Winter.

Food

Do not feed. Split Rock self-feeds.

Pruning & Grooming

Split Rock will produce new leaves to replace old ones and they feed on the old leaves, so do not remove.

Grow More Plants

Propagation can be achieved by cutting a single leaf from a plant before the new leaves appear. Let this cutting dry for a few days and then plant in the same way as mature plants, as described above.

STAGHORN FERN

Platycerium spp.

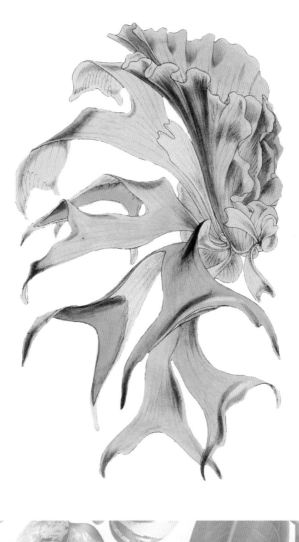

Meanings
goals, desire, confidence, optimism, anticipation

Uses
Staghorn Ferns live so well in bathrooms, and there they can be hung near mirrors so that they reflect their energies of hope and optimism upon those going about their morning preparations. Mounting on trees near front doors and gates will help set paths to goals and desires. Give to another to say, 'Good luck', 'I wish you good times and success' or 'I believe in you'.

CARE
houseplant maintenance level = challenging

Profile
The spectacular Staghorn Fern is a tropical epiphyte from Africa, South America, South-East Asia, New Guinea, and Australia. They grow in the wild by attaching themselves high up in trees, where their deep green antler-shaped fronds reach out from their rooted position against the trunk of the host tree. Staghorn Fern can attain a width of 1m (39") and some species form a crown with their uppermost fronds in order to catch rain and falling forest debris. Non-toxic to humans and animals.

Container & Soil
They can be grown in a pot, but look magnificent when mounted on bark and displayed on a wall, or even attached to a tree. Use an orchid compost-based soil for best results.

Position & Light
Staghorn Ferns prefer filtered bright light and high humidity so are the perfect bathroom houseplant. If growing in pots, stand the pots on trays filled with wet pebbles. If you decide to grow many Staghorn Ferns, a humidifier and auto-misting irrigation is helpful (dependent on position in the home).

Water

Care needs to be taken to not over-water because rot can occur, but they do need their water needs carefully monitored. Allow the top of the soil to dry out between watering, but water when the bottom leaves start to feel dry. This can be done by submerging the whole plant in water for 15 minutes. As the plant absorbs water through its fronds and requires a high humidity, mist regularly.

Food

Feed with a liquid fertiliser once a month from mid-Spring through to early Autumn (fall). For the rest of the year feeding won't be necessary.

Pruning & Grooming

As they age, the lower fronds will turn brown. These should not be removed as they provide support for the plant. Let them fall naturally. If growing in pots, re-pot every two to three years and replace the soil when you do. For bushy growth, remove the growing tips.

Grow More Plants

New plants can be created by removing the growing tips and planting in an orchid-specific potting mix. Keep in a bright, filtered light-position, and water well.

TAIL FLOWER

Anthurium andraeanum

Meanings
comfort, cheer, unity, integrity, passion

Uses
Placed in a bedroom, Tail Flower can improve relationships. In the entrance area of any space, the plant will induce a hospitable atmosphere, and happiness. Invite into areas where business meetings take place to ensure that all within are working with integrity and revealing their true motivations. Give to another to say, 'You are welcome here', 'I love you' or 'I wish you happiness'.

CARE
houseplant maintenance level = average

Profile
The leathery, deep dark-green heart-shaped leaves of the Tail Flower plant are often overlooked in favour of its well-known flowers, but they are a beautiful feature themselves of this Colombian and Ecuadorian native. Its waxy flowers are made up of a glossy spathe of either reds, pinks, whites or burgundy, and its long spadix are covered in tiny flowers. Indoors, the plant usually attains a size of 45 x 30cm (18 x 12"). The whole plant is toxic, and the sap is a skin irritant, so care must be taken with its exposure to humans and animals.

Container & Soil
Select a container that is a size larger than the plant. Use a mix of half compost-based soil to half good-quality potting mix and add broken pots or large stones in the bottom to provide extra drainage. When planting, leave the root ball just above the soil level and cover with moss to protect it.

Position & Light

Bright though indirect light and a warm draught-free position without fluctuating temperatures is essential. Humidity needs to be about average, but high humidity will encourage flowering.

Water

Only water when the top soil becomes dry, and do so very sparingly. Stand on a tray or saucer of wet pebbles and mist a few times a week.

Food

Use a slow-release fertiliser once every six months and then from mid-Spring until late Summer use a liquid fertiliser (potash-based) at half strength once every two weeks.

Pruning & Grooming

Re-pot when necessary – preferably in Spring but only when the plant is root-bound. Replace the soil completely when you do so.

Grow More Plants

New plants can be created by division. When re-potting in Spring, separate sections that contain a growth point and fleshy roots. Pot in a mixture of half peat moss and half indoor potting mix or a commercial seed- and cutting-raising mixture. Place in a warm position and water sparingly.

TASSEL FERN

Huperzia spp.

Meanings
self-preservation, regeneration, security, interconnectedness, reconciliation

Uses
Tassel Fern is supportive of those who work in fields that connect people with each other. The plant offers its own healing and wholeness and provides feelings of security and self-preservation. Place in or near bedrooms to promote peaceful and regenerative sleep. When times have been difficult, Tassel Fern will help with reconciliation and healing. Give to another to say, 'I am sorry', 'I forgive you' or 'Let's start again'.

CARE
houseplant maintenance level = average

Profile
With its interesting cascading tassels of green foliage, Tassel Fern makes for an unusual and soft feature. The Tassel Fern is a very slow-growing plant and its connection to the fossils of other ferns and clubmosses has enabled us to date the Tassel Fern back to millions of years ago. They are found in the wild in Australia, Asia, North America and India. Mildly toxic to humans and animals if ingested.

Container & Soil
They can be grown in hanging baskets or a standard pot if you allow room for the plant to tumble over the sides. As they are an epiphyte, most species will do best in an open bark mix such as a commercial orchid mix.

Position & Light
Tassel Fern will require a shaded position, high humidity and good airflow.

Water

Never allow this plant to dry out, growing medium must always remain moist but not waterlogged.

Food

From mid-Spring until mid-Summer, supplement with a liquid fertiliser at half strength. Never use any fertilisers that contain chemicals.

Pruning & Grooming

There is nothing that needs to be done especially, but care should be taken that tassels are not in danger of being damaged as they grow. Re-pot in the Spring if they outgrow their container.

Grow More Plants

Stem cuttings are perhaps the easiest way to try and propagate this plant, but it is a notoriously challenging task. Take tip cuttings during Spring and plant in the same growing medium as mature plants. Some Tassel Ferns will also produce plantlets and these can be removed with a sharp knife and planted in the same manner.

COMMUNITY
UMBRELLA TREE
Schefflera arboricola

Meanings
community, guidance, secrets, care, stability, protection

Uses
This plant is a very good selection for offices, work spaces, commercial lobbies and home living spaces in which many people are working, living and moving through. The Umbrella Tree provides a sense of community and togetherness, and provides stability. The Umbrella Tree is also a natural air cleanser, especially of benzene. Give to another to say, 'I wish you well with work', 'Happy job hunting' or 'I'm here for you'.

CARE
houseplant maintenance level = easy

Profile
Glossy almond-shaped olive-green leaves fan around each branching stem to form 'umbrellas', which gives this plant its popular common name. In the wild, this plant can attain a height of 4m (13ft) but grown indoors they usually only reach between 1.5–2.4m (5–8ft). They are toxic to cats, dogs and humans, if ingested, plus the sap is a skin irritant, so care should be taken with position.

Container & Soil
The most important thing you can do for your Umbrella Tree is to ensure a very free-draining soil and container. It grows best in a mixture of one-part coarse sand to two-parts compost-rich potting mix.

Position & Light
Low to bright filtered light works well. Avoid direct sunlight, especially positions right next to windows that receive a lot of full sun. Tolerates air-conditioning and heating well.

Water

Take care not to over-water and let the top layer of soil dry out between watering. The atmosphere can be of a medium humidity, or even a little dry.

Food

The Umbrella Tree will do very well with an extra boost from early Spring through to late Autumn (fall) with a liquid fertiliser made up to half the recommended strength, once every two weeks.

Pruning & Grooming

Pruning of new growth tips will encourage the plant to thicken. Watch for yellow leaves: this means you are over-watering. Re-pot every second year in the warmer part of Spring and replace the soil when you do so. Clean leaves regularly with a damp cloth and you may find your plant benefits by staking, to hold up stems.

Grow More Plants

Take terminal cuttings in Spring of between 10–15cm (4–6") and have no more than three leaves on each. Place in a glass of distilled or rain water and leave on a warm sunny windowsill or similar. They should take root in two to three months. Then plant out as suggest above.

VENUS FLY TRAP

Dionaea muscipula

Meanings
attraction, manifestation, certainty, awareness, protection

Uses
Place a Venus Fly Trap on your desk, kitchen bench or any place that you spend a lot of time, to help sharpen your intuition and awareness. If you are meditating, this plant helps deepen experiences. In a work environment, the Venus Fly Trap will assist with manifestation and decision-making and, as the name suggests, the plant will be very helpful in matters of the heart. Have one around to attract love. Give to another to say, 'I want you!', 'I understand' or 'May your wishes come true'.

CARE
houseplant maintenance level = moderate

Profile
The Venus Fly Trap's apple-green leaves, edged with what appears to be tiny teeth, open wide like a jaw and then slam shut on its prey: tiny insects. This eastern United States native produces two types of leaves and both are traps, but most grow close to the centre of the plant. In the warmer Summer months, some will develop to become longer and shaded in a light red tone. The plant will usually grow to a size of 10 x 20cm (4 x 8") and produce white tubular flowers. Non-toxic to humans and animals.

Container & Soil
Choose a pot that it is only slightly bigger than the plant. Plant in a mixture of half perlite and half sphagnum moss. Never use potting soil or compost, which will kill your plant.

Position & Light
The Venus Fly Trap will require a sunny spot and must be set outside occasionally or put on an open window sill so the plant can catch insects.

Water

From early Spring through to late Summer, set the pot in a tray or saucer of water (it must be rainwater or distilled water) so it can draw water this way. Do not stand it in water for the rest of the year; rather, water lightly and avoid wetting the foliage when the soil starts to become dry.

Food

Never feed this plant any fertiliser. It is also best not to hand feed the plant. Hand feeding too much will kill the plant.

Pruning & Grooming

Re-pot the plant every year in very early Spring, and renew growing medium. Venus Fly Trap will go into dormancy throughout Winter and you will need to keep it in a cooler place indoors. Pinch out flowers when they appear to encourage stronger foliage (traps) growth.

Grow More Plants

The easiest way to propagate a Venus Fly Trap is via division. Second to multiple points will usually form. Leaves will become crowded and a second rosette of leaves will form. Wait until Spring, and then when you re-pot your plant, gently pull the new growth to separate and re-pot the new growth.

BALANCE
ZEBRA PLANT
Aphelandra squarrosa

Meanings

time, temperance, harmony, management, moderation

Uses

The Zebra Plant will help with brainstorming ideas, balancing power within relationships and situations so that a harmonious outcome or environment can be created, and stimulating mental processes and creativity, when stagnation has occurred. If humid enough, the Zebra Plant will provide all these energies in a work area. Having one in a bathroom is ideal so that you can focus on the plant each morning and set out balanced and ready for inspiration.

CARE

houseplant maintenance level = challenging

Profile

The Zebra Plant's joyous sunny flower stalk that appears in Autumn (fall) earns it another common name: 'Saffron Spike'. This spike is covered in yellow bracts that surround and hold the orange blossoms within. Zebra Plant originates from the Atlantic Forest of Brazil and the deep green and cream leaves are usually 20–30cm (9–12") in length, with the plant growing to about 45cm (18") in height. The wonderful thing about this plant is that it is non-toxic to people and animals, although the sap can be a skin irritant. Non-toxic to humans and animals.

Container & Soil

Place in a container just a little larger than the plant and use a very rich compost-based soil. In the Spring, re-pot and replace soil yearly, going up a size or two if required.

Position & Light

Zebra Plant likes bright filtered light, but not in direct sun, and medium to high humidity. They grow very well if you place their pots on saucers or trays filled with wet pebbles.

Water

You must ensure that you only use rainwater or distilled water because this plant is very sensitive to chemicals. Never let the soil dry out. Misting daily will help keep humidity high.

Food

They only require feeding from mid-Spring through to the end of Summer and this is best achieved with a full-strength liquid fertiliser once every two weeks.

Pruning & Grooming

To keep growth compact and tidy, the bottom few leaves should be removed and the flower stalk pruned once it is spent.

Grow More Plants

Take tip cuttings in mid- to late Spring and plant into the potting mixture suggested above. Water, then place in a mini greenhouse or cover with plastic to keep humidity high. Leave cover on and do not water again. Plants should root in about six weeks.

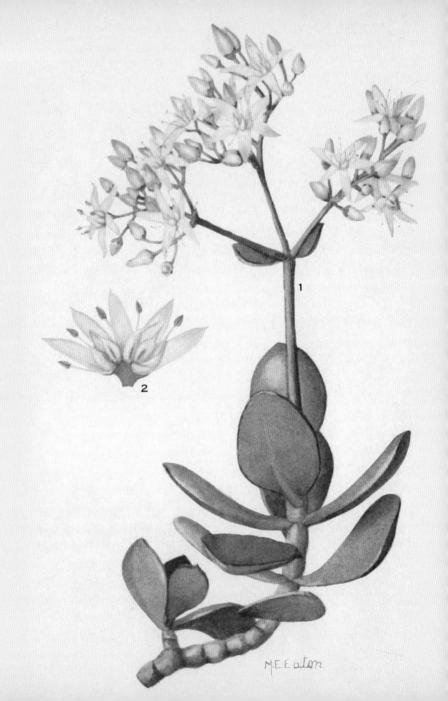

1

2

M.E.Eaton

HOUSEPLANT RESOURCES

MEANINGS AND THEIR HOUSEPLANTS

A

abundance: Crown of Thorns
(*Euphorbia milii*), Desert Rose
(*Adenium obesum*),
Jade Plant (*Crassula ovata*), Money
Tree (*Pachira aquatica*),
Boston Fern (*Nephrolepis exaltata*)

acceptance: Air Plant (*Tillandsia spp.*)

accomplishment: Jade Plant (*Crassula ovata*)

action: Bamboo Palm (*Rhapis excelsa*),
Fruit Salad Plant (*Monstera deliciosa*),
Rubber Plant (*Ficus elastica*)

adaptation: Air Plant (*Tillandsia spp.*),
Golden Cane Palm (*Dypsis lutescens*)

advancement: Flaming Katy (*Kalanchoe blossfeldiana*)

affection: Queen of Hearts
(*Homalomena spp.*)

affirmation: Flaming Sword (*Vriesea splendens*)

alignment: Golden Cane Palm (*Dypsis lutescens*)

anticipation: Staghorn Fern
(*Platycerium spp.*)

appreciation: Heart Leaf (*Philodendron hederaceum*)

argument: Arrowhead Plant
(*Syngonium podophyllum*)

attraction: Venus Fly Trap (*Dionaea muscipula*)

attainment: Arrowhead Plant
(*Syngonium podophyllum*)

awakening: Painted Leaves
(*Plectranthus scutellarioides*)

awareness: Haworthia (*Haworthia spp.*),
Venus Fly Trap (*Dionaea muscipula*)

B

balance: Fiddle-leaf Fig (*Ficus lyrata*),
Zebra Plant (*Aphelandra squarrosa*),
Peace Lily (*Spathiphyllum wallisii*)

beginnings: Arrowhead Plant
(*Syngonium podophyllum*)

bind: Devil's Ivy (*Epipremnum aureum*)

blessing, family: Chain of Hearts
(*Ceropegia woodii*)

blessing, home: Chain of Hearts
(*Ceropegia woodii*)

breath: Bird's Nest Fern (*Asplenium nidus*)

C

care: Umbrella Tree *(Schefflera arboricola)*, Queen of Hearts *(Homalomena spp.)*

calmness: Air Plant *(Tillandsia spp.)*, Peace Lily *(Spathiphyllum wallisii)*, Hens and Chicks *(Sempervivum tectorum)*

capture: Devil's Ivy *(Epipremnum aureum)*

centre: Crown of Thorns *(Euphorbia milii)*

certainty: Venus Fly Trap *(Dionaea muscipula)*

change: Croton *(Codiaeum variegatum)*

cheer: Tail Flower *(Anthurium andraeanum)*

clarity: Air Plant *(Tillandsia spp.)*, Hens and Chicks *(Sempervivum tectorum)*

cleansing: Peace Lily *(Spathiphyllum wallisii)*

clearing: Haworthia *(Haworthia spp.)*

comfort: Tail Flower *(Anthurium andraeanum)*

commitment, romantic: Chain of Hearts *(Ceropegia woodii)*

communication: Air Plant *(Tillandsia spp.)*, Moth Orchid *(Phalaenopsis spp.)*

community: Umbrella Tree *(Schefflera arboricola)*

compassion: Moth Orchid *(Phalaenopsis spp.)*, Queen of Hearts *(Homalomena spp.)*

consciousness: Moth Orchid *(Phalaenopsis spp.)*, Rainbow Pincushion *(Mammillaria rhodantha)*

confidence: Christmas Cactus *(Schlumbergera truncata)*, Staghorn Fern *(Platycerium spp.)*, Flaming Sword *(Vriesea splendens)*

connection: English Ivy *(Hedera helix)*

contentment: Jade Plant *(Crassula ovata)*

creativity: Begonia *(Begonia spp.)*, Snake Plant *(Sansevieria trifasciata)*, Spider Plant *(Chlorophytum comosum)*

D

decision: Bamboo Palm *(Rhapis excelsa)*

dedication: Peace Lily *(Spathiphyllum wallisii)*

deflection: Haworthia *(Haworthia spp.)*

defence: Flaming Sword *(Vriesea splendens)*

delay: Devil's Ivy *(Epipremnum aureum)*

desire: Staghorn Fern *(Platycerium spp.)*, Devil's Ivy *(Epipremnum aureum)*

destiny: Elephant Ear *(Alocasia x amazonica)*

determination: Bamboo Palm *(Rhapis excelsa)*

detox: Flaming Sword *(Vriesea splendens)*

development: Croton *(Codiaeum variegatum)*

devotion: Chain of Hearts *(Ceropegia woodii)*, Heart Leaf *(Philodendron hederaceum)* direction: African Violet *(Saintpaulia spp.)*, Bamboo Palm *(Rhapis excelsa)*, Boston Fern *(Nephrolepis exaltata)*, Maidenhair Fern *(Adiantum raddianum)*

dream: Painted Leaves *(Plectranthus scutellarioides)*

E

education: Croton *(Codiaeum variegatum)*

emotion: Rainbow Pincushion *(Mammillaria rhodantha)*, Queen of Hearts *(Homalomena spp.)*

ending obsession: Air Plant *(Tillandsia spp.)*

endings: Begonia *(Begonia spp.)*

endurance: Split Rock *(Pleiospilos nelii)*

eternity: Hens and Chicks *(Sempervivum tectorum)*

exuberance: Rubber Plant *(Ficus elastica)*

expansion: Fruit Salad Plant *(Monstera deliciosa)*

expression: Maidenhair Fern *(Adiantum raddianum)*

F

faith: Prayer Plant *(Maranta leuconeura)*

family: Desert Rose *(Adenium obesum)*

family blessing: Chain of Hearts *(Ceropegia woodii)*

fertility: Chain of Hearts *(Ceropegia woodii)*, Desert Rose *(Adenium obesum)*, English Ivy *(Hedera helix)*

fidelity: English Ivy *(Hedera helix)*

finances: Jade Plant *(Crassula ovata)*

flexibility: Snake Plant *(Sansevieria trifasciata)*

focus: Rubber Plant *(Ficus elastica)*

forgiveness: Tassel Fern *(Huperzia spp.)*

fortune: Elephant Ear *(Alocasia x amazonica)*

freedom: Elephant Ear *(Alocasia x amazonica)*, Rainbow Pincushion *(Mammillaria rhodantha)*

G

goals: Staghorn Fern *(Platycerium spp.)*

grief: Aloe Vera *(Aloe barbadensis miller)*

grounding: Flaming Katy *(Kalanchoe blossfeldiana)*

growth: Fruit Salad Plant *(Monstera deliciosa)*, Heart Leaf *(Philodendron hederaceum)*, Elephant Ear *(Alocasia x amazonica)*

guidance: Umbrella Tree *(Schefflera arboricola)*

H

happiness: Money Tree *(Pachira aquatica)*, Heart Leaf *(Philodendron hederaceum)*

harmony: Crown of Thorns *(Euphorbia milii)*, Fiddle-leaf Fig *(Ficus lyrata)*, Zebra Plant *(Aphelandra squarrosa)*

healing: Aloe Vera *(Aloe barbadensis miller)*, Christmas Cactus *(Schlumbergera truncata)*, Peace Lily *(Spathiphyllum wallisii)*, Snake Plant *(Sansevieria trifasciata)*, Spider Plant *(Chlorophytum comosum)*

higher learning: African Violet
(*Saintpaulia spp.*)

home blessing: Chain of Hearts
(*Ceropegia woodii*)

honour: Fruit Salad Plant (*Monstera deliciosa*)

hospitality: Tail Flower (*Anthurium andraeanum*)

hope: Prayer Plant (*Maranta leuconeura*), Staghorn Fern
(*Platycerium spp.*)

I

ideas, new: Arrowhead Plant
(*Syngonium podophyllum*)

illumination: Rainbow Pincushion
(*Mammillaria rhodantha*)

imitation: Painted Leaves (*Plectranthus scutellarioides*)

immortality: English Ivy (*Hedera helix*)

independence: Jade Plant (*Crassula ovata*), Spider Plant (*Chlorophytum comosum*)

inspiration: Arrowhead Plant
(*Syngonium podophyllum*)

integrity: Tail Flower (*Anthurium andraeanum*)

intention: Spider Plant (*Chlorophytum comosum*)

interconnectedness: Tassel Fern
(*Huperzia spp.*)

interest: Rubber Plant (*Ficus elastica*)

intimacy: Christmas Cactus
(*Schlumbergera truncata*)

intuition: Venus Fly Trap (*Dionaea muscipula*), Flaming Sword (*Vriesea splendens*)

L

longevity: Cast-Iron Plant (*Aspidistra elatior*)

love: Chain of Hearts (*Ceropegia woodii*), Christmas Cactus (*Schlumbergera truncata*),
Heart Leaf (*Philodendron hederaceum*)

love, unconditional: Crown of Thorns
(*Euphorbia milii*)

luck: Chain of Hearts (*Ceropegia woodii*), Desert Rose (*Adenium obesum*),
Jade Plant (*Crassula ovata*), Money Tree (*Pachira aquatica*),
Boston Fern (*Nephrolepis exaltata*)

M

management: Zebra Plant (*Aphelandra squarrosa*)

manifestation: Venus Fly Trap (*Dionaea muscipula*)

meditation: Prayer Plant (*Maranta leuconeura*),
Rainbow Pincushion (*Mammillaria rhodantha*)

memory: Painted Leaves (*Plectranthus scutellarioides*)

mending: Split Rock (*Pleiospilos nelii*)

mindfulness: Air Plant (*Tillandsia spp.*), Spider Plant (*Chlorophytum comosum*)

moderation: Zebra Plant (*Aphelandra squarrosa*)

money: Money Tree (*Pachira aquatica*)

move: Croton (*Codiaeum variegatum*)

movement: Bamboo Palm *(Rhapis excelsa)*

N

negativity, removal of: Begonia *(Begonia spp.)*
new ideas: Arrowhead Plant *(Syngonium podophyllum)*
nurturing: Queen of Hearts *(Homalomena spp.)*

O

obtain: Devil's Ivy *(Epipremnum aureum)*
obsession, ending: Air Plant *(Tillandsia spp.)*
obstacles: Split Rock *(Pleiospilos nelii)*
opportunity: Fruit Salad Plant *(Monstera deliciosa)*, Elephant Ear *(Alocasia x amazonica)*
optimism: Staghorn Fern *(Platycerium spp.)*

P

partnerships: Fiddle-leaf Fig *(Ficus lyrata)*
passion: Heart Leaf *(Philodendron hederaceum)*, Tail Flower *(Anthurium andraeanum)*
peace: Prayer Plant *(Maranta leuconeura)*, Moth Orchid *(Phalaenopsis spp.)*
plans: Fruit Salad Plant *(Monstera deliciosa)*
positivity: Bird's Nest Fern *(Asplenium nidus)*, Split Rock *(Pleiospilos nelii)*

preservation: Bird's Nest Fern *(Asplenium nidus)*
prevention: Haworthia *(Haworthia spp.)*
pride: Cast-Iron Plant *(Aspidistra elatior)*
progress: Bamboo Palm *(Rhapis excelsa)*
prosperity: Desert Rose *(Adenium obesum)*, Money Tree *(Pachira aquatica)*, Devil's Ivy *(Epipremnum aureum)*
protection: African Violet *(Saintpaulia spp.)*, Cast-Iron Plant *(Aspidistra elatior)*, Umbrella Tree *(Schefflera arboricola)*, English Ivy *(Hedera helix)*, Haworthia *(Haworthia spp.)*, Bird's Nest Fern *(Asplenium nidus)*, Venus Fly Trap *(Dionaea muscipula)*, Spider Plant *(Chlorophytum comosum)*, Boston Fern *(Nephrolepis exaltata)*, Hens and Chicks *(Sempervivum tectorum)*, Maidenhair Fern *(Adiantum raddianum)*
purification: Peace Lily *(Spathiphyllum wallisii)*, Hens and Chicks *(Sempervivum tectorum)*
purpose: Maidenhair Fern *(Adiantum raddianum)*

Q

quiet: Fiddle-leaf Fig *(Ficus lyrata)*

R

rebirth: Elephant Ear *(Alocasia x amazonica)*

reconciliation: Tassel Fern *(Huperzia spp.)*

reflection: Split Rock *(Pleiospilos nelii)*

regeneration: Aloe Vera *(Aloe barbadensis miller)*, Tassel Fern *(Huperzia spp.)*

reinforcement: Flaming Katy *(Kalanchoe blossfeldiana)*

relationships: Fiddle-leaf Fig *(Ficus lyrata)*

relaxation: Prayer Plant *(Maranta leuconeura)*

removal of negativity: Begonia *(Begonia spp.)*

renewal: Aloe Vera *(Aloe barbadensis miller)*

resilience: Flaming Katy *(Kalanchoe blossfeldiana)*

restoration: Aloe Vera *(Aloe barbadensis miller)*, Rubber Plant *(Ficus elastica)*

reversal: Haworthia *(Haworthia spp.)*

revision: Croton *(Codiaeum variegatum)*

reward: Golden Cane Palm *(Dypsis lutescens)*

romantic commitments: Chain of Hearts *(Ceropegia woodii)*

S

secrets: Umbrella Tree *(Schefflera arboricola)*

security: Tassel Fern *(Huperzia spp.)*

self-confidence: African Violet *(Saintpaulia spp.)*

self-forgiveness: Crown of Thorns *(Euphorbia milii)*

self-expression: Maidenhair Fern *(Adiantum raddianum)*

self-preservation: Tassel Fern *(Huperzia spp.)*

self-respect: Cast-Iron Plant *(Aspidistra elatior)*, Bird's Nest Fern *(Asplenium nidus)*

sensitivity: Maidenhair Fern *(Adiantum raddianum)*

sensuality: Moth Orchid *(Phalaenopsis spp.)*

separateness: Split Rock *(Pleiospilos nelii)*

sexuality: Christmas Cactus *(Schlumbergera truncata)*

shield: Moth Orchid *(Phalaenopsis spp.)*

sincerity: Boston Fern *(Nephrolepis exaltata)*

sleep: Painted Leaves *(Plectranthus scutellarioides)*

spirituality: African Violet *(Saintpaulia spp.)*, Prayer Plant *(Maranta leuconeura)*

stability: Umbrella Tree *(Schefflera arboricola)*, Flaming Katy *(Kalanchoe blossfeldiana)*

stress reduction: Arrowhead Plant *(Syngonium podophyllum)*

strength: Snake Plant *(Sansevieria trifasciata)*, Golden Cane Palm *(Dypsis lutescens)*

success: Bamboo Palm *(Rhapis excelsa)*, Desert Rose *Adenium obesum)*, Money Tree *(Pachira aquatica)*, Golden Cane Palm *(Dypsis lutescens)*

study: Rubber Plant *(Ficus elastica)*
survival: Aloe Vera *(Aloe barbadensis miller)*, Hens and Chicks *(Sempervivum tectorum)*

T
technology: Snake Plant *(Sansevieria trifasciata)*
temperance: Zebra Plant *(Aphelandra squarrosa)*
time: Zebra Plant *(Aphelandra squarrosa)*
tenacity: English Ivy *(Hedera helix)*
togetherness: Christmas Cactus *(Schlumbergera truncata)*
transition: Begonia *(Begonia spp.)*
transformation: Croton *(Codiaeum variegatum)*
truth: Snake Plant *(Sansevieria trifasciata)*, Boston Fern *(Nephrolepis exaltata)*,
    Flaming Sword *(Vriesea splendens)*

U
unconditional love: Crown of Thorns *(Euphorbia milii)*
understanding: Fiddle-leaf Fig *(Ficus lyrata)*

unity: Tail Flower *(Anthurium andraeanum)*

V
victory: Golden Cane Palm *(Dypsis lutescens)*
visions: Painted Leaves *(Plectranthus scutellarioides)*
vulnerability: Queen of Hearts *(Homalomena spp.)*

W
warning: Begonia *(Begonia spp.)*
wealth: Desert Rose *(Adenium obesum)*
wellness: Bird's Nest Fern *(Asplenium nidus)*
wholeness: Rainbow Pincushion *(Mammillaria rhodantha)*
willpower: Bamboo Palm *(Rhapis excelsa)*
wishes: Chain of Hearts *(Ceropegia woodii)*
work: Cast-Iron Plant *(Aspidistra elatior)*

Y
youth: Arrowhead Plant *(Syngonium podophyllum)*

ANNIVERSARY HOUSEPLANTS

1st Aloe Vera *(Aloe barbadensis miller),* Arrowhead Plant *(Syngonium podophyllum),* Flaming Sword *(Vriesea splendens)*

2nd Heart Leaf *(Philodendron hederaceum)*

3rd Peace Lily *(Spathiphyllum wallisii),* Snake Plant *(Sansevieria trifasciata)*

4th Rubber Plant *(Ficus elastica)*, Hens and Chicks *(Sempervivum tectorum)*

5th Umbrella Tree *(Schefflera arboricola),* Maidenhair Fern *(Adiantum raddianum)*

6th Fiddle-leaf Fig *(Ficus lyrata),* Tassel Fern *(Huperzia spp.)*

7th Bamboo Palm *(Rhapis excelsa),* Queen of Hearts *(Homalomena spp.),* Split Rock *(Pleiospilos nelii)*

8th Jade Plant *(Crassula ovata),* Staghorn Fern *(Platycerium spp.)*

9th African Violet *(Saintpaulia spp.),* Money Tree *(Pachira aquatica)*

10th Croton *(Codiaeum variegatum),* Crown of Thorns *(Euphorbia milii)*

11th Air Plant *(Tillandsia spp.),* English Ivy *(Hedera helix)*

12th Christmas Cactus *(Schlumbergera truncate)*

13th Begonia *(Begonia spp.)*

14th Cast-Iron Plant *(Aspidistra elatior),* Moth Orchid *(Phalaenopsis spp.)*

15th Haworthia *(Haworthia spp.)*

16th Chain of Hearts *(Ceropegia woodii)*

17th Desert Rose *(Adenium obesum),* Prayer Plant *(Maranta leuconeura)*

18th Fruit Salad Plant *(Monstera deliciosa),* Rainbow Pincushion *(Mammillaria rhodantha)*

19th Venus Fly Trap *(Dionaea muscipula),* Queen of Hearts *(Homalomena spp.)*

20th Zebra Plant *(Aphelandra squarrosa),* Split Rock *(Pleiospilos nelii)*

21st: Flaming Sword *(Vriesea splendens),* Maidenhair Fern *(Adiantum raddianum)*

25th Devil's Ivy *(Epipremnum aureum),* Elephant Ear *(Alocasia x amazonica)*

30th Bird's Nest Fern *(Asplenium nidus),* Painted Leaves *(Plectranthus scutellarioides)*

40th Tail Flower *(Anthurium andraeanum)*

50th Golden Cane Palm *(Dypsis lutescens),* Spider Plant *(Chlorophytum comosum),* Boston Fern *(Nephrolepis exaltata)*

HOUSEPLANTS FOR DAYS OF THE WEEK

Monday
Arrowhead Plant *(Syngonium podophyllum)*
Venus Fly Trap *(Dionaea muscipula)*
Elephant Ear *(Alocasia x amazonica)*
Tassel Fern *(Huperzia spp.)*

Tuesday
Bamboo Palm *(Rhapis excelsa)*
Snake Plant *(Sansevieria trifasciata)*
Split Rock *(Pleiospilos nelii)*

Wednesday
Air Plant *(Tillandsia spp.)*
Croton *(Codiaeum variegatum)*
Zebra Plant *(Aphelandra squarrosa)*
Staghorn Fern *(Platycerium spp.)*
Moth Orchid *(Phalaenopsis spp.)*
Rubber Plant *(Ficus elastica)*
Flaming Sword *(Vriesea splendens)*
Maidenhair Fern *(Adiantum raddianum)*

Thursday
Desert Rose *(Adenium obesum)*
Jade Plant *(Crassula ovata)*
Peace Lily *(Spathiphyllum wallisii)*
Money Tree *(Pachira aquatica)*
Bird's Nest Fern *(Asplenium nidus)*
Boston Fern *(Nephrolepis exaltata)*

Friday
Fiddle-leaf Fig *(Ficus lyrata)*
Chain of Hearts *(Ceropegia woodii)*
Christmas Cactus *(Schlumbergera truncata)*
Crown of Thorns *(Euphorbia milii)*
Heart Leaf *(Philodendron hederaceum)*
Tail Flower *(Anthurium andraeanum)*
Painted Leaves *(Plectranthus scutellarioides)*
Queen of Hearts *(Homalomena spp.)*

Saturday
Begonia *(Begonia spp.)*
Umbrella Tree *(Schefflera arboricola)*
Haworthia *(Haworthia spp.)*
Devil's Ivy *(Epipremnum aureum)*
Spider Plant *(Chlorophytum comosum)*
Hens and Chicks *(Sempervivum tectorum)*
Maidenhair Fern *(Adiantum raddianum)*
Rainbow Pincushion *(Mammillaria rhodantha)*

Sunday
African Violet *(Saintpaulia spp.)*
Aloe Vera *(Aloe barbadensis miller)*
Cast-Iron Plant *(Aspidistra elatior)*
Fruit Salad Plant *(Monstera deliciosa)*
Prayer Plant *(Maranta leuconeura)*
Golden Cane Palm *(Dypsis lutescens)*

HOUSEPLANTS OF EACH MONTH

January
Arrowhead Plant *(Syngonium podophyllum)*
Moth Orchid *(Phalaenopsis spp.)*
Maidenhair Fern *(Adiantum raddianum)*

February
Desert Rose *(Adenium obesum)*
Prayer Plant *(Maranta leuconeura)*
Painted Leaves *(Plectranthus scutellarioides)*
Queen of Hearts *(Homalomena spp.)*

March
Staghorn Fern *(Platycerium spp.)*
Rubber Plant *(Ficus elastica)*
Golden Cane Palm *(Dypsis lutescens)*
Hens and Chicks *(Sempervivum tectorum)*

April
Aloe Vera *(Aloe barbadensis miller)*
Crown of Thorns *(Euphorbia milii)*
Bird's Nest Fern *(Asplenium nidus)*

May
Jade Plant *(Crassula ovata)*
Umbrella Tree *(Schefflera arboricola)*
Spider Plant *(Chlorophytum comosum)*

June
Fiddle-leaf Fig *(Ficus lyrata)*
Chain of Hearts *(Ceropegia woodii)*
Heart Leaf *(Philodendron hederaceum)*

July
Bamboo Palm *(Rhapis excelsa)*
Fruit Salad Plant *(Monstera deliciosa)*
Peace Lily *(Spathiphyllum wallisii)*
Snake Plant *(Sansevieria trifasciata)*

August
Cast-Iron Plant *(Aspidistra elatior)*
Venus Fly Trap *(Dionaea muscipula)*
Tail Flower *(Anthurium andraeanum)*
Flaming Sword *(Vriesea splendens)*

September
African Violet *(Saintpaulia spp.)*
Haworthia *(Haworthia spp.)*
Boston Fern *(Nephrolepis exaltata)*

October
Air Plant *(Tillandsia spp.)*
Zebra Plant *(Aphelandra squarrosa)*
Devil's Ivy *(Epipremnum aureum)*
Split Rock *(Pleiospilos nelii)*
Tassel Fern *(Huperzia spp.)*

November
Begonia *(Begonia spp.)*
Croton *(Codiaeum variegatum)*
English Ivy *(Hedera helix)*
Rainbow Pincushion *(Mammillaria rhodantha)*

December
Christmas Cactus *(Schlumbergera truncata)*
Money Tree *(Pachira aquatica)*
Elephant Ear *(Alocasia x amazonica)*

HOUSEPLANTS OF THE ZODIAC

Aquarius 20th January – 18th February
Arrowhead Plant *(Syngonium podophyllum)*
Desert Rose *(Adenium obesum)*
Prayer Plant *(Maranta leuconeura)*
Moth Orchid *(Phalaenopsis spp.)*
Maidenhair Fern *(Adiantum raddianum)*

Pisces 19th February – 20th March
Staghorn Fern *(Platycerium spp.)*
Rubber Plant *(Ficus elastica)*
Painted Leaves *(Plectranthus scutellarioides)*
Queen of Hearts *(Homalomena spp.)*

Aries 21st March – 19th April
Aloe Vera *(Aloe barbadensis miller)*
Bird's Nest Fern *(Asplenium nidus)*
Golden Cane Palm *(Dypsis lutescens)*
Hens and Chicks *(Sempervivum tectorum)*

Taurus 20th April – 20th May
Jade Plant *(Crassula ovata)*
Umbrella Tree *(Schefflera arboricola)*
Spider Plant *(Chlorophytum comosum)*

Gemini 21st May – 20th June
Fiddle-leaf Fig *(Ficus lyrata)*
Chain of Hearts *(Ceropegia woodii)*
Crown of Thorns *(Euphorbia milii)*
Heart Leaf *(Philodendron hederaceum)*

Cancer 21st June – 22 July
Bamboo Palm *(Rhapis excelsa)*
Peace Lily *(Spathiphyllum wallisii)*
Snake Plant *(Sansevieria trifasciata)*

Leo 23rd July – 22nd August
Cast-Iron Plant *(Aspidistra elatior)*
Fruit Salad Plant *(Monstera deliciosa)*
Tail Flower *(Anthurium andraeanum)*
Flaming Sword *(Vriesea splendens)*

Virgo 23rd August – 22 September
African Violet *(Saintpaulia spp.)*
Haworthia *(Haworthia spp.)*
Venus Fly Trap *(Dionaea muscipula)*

Libra 23rd September – 22nd October
Air Plant *(Tillandsia spp.)*
Zebra Plant *(Aphelandra squarrosa)*
Boston Fern *(Nephrolepis exaltata)*

Scorpio 23rd October – 21st November
Begonia *(Begonia spp.)*
Devil's Ivy *(Epipremnum aureum)*
Split Rock *(Pleiospilos nelii)*
Tassel Fern *(Huperzia spp.)*

Sagittarius 22nd November – 21st December
Croton *(Codiaeum variegatum)*
English Ivy *(Hedera helix)*
Rainbow Pincushion *(Mammillaria rhodantha)*

Capricorn 22nd December – 19th January

Christmas Cactus *(Schlumbergera truncata)*

Money Tree *(Pachira aquatica)*
Elephant Ear *(Alocasia x amazonica)*

HOUSEPLANTS OF THE MOON PHASES

Waxing Moon
Aloe Vera *(Aloe barbadensis miller)*
Arrowhead Plant *(Syngonium podophyllum)*
Bamboo Palm *(Rhapis excelsa)*
Croton *(Codiaeum variegatum)*
Fruit Salad Plant *(Monstera deliciosa)*
Jade Plant *(Crassula ovata)*
Snake Plant *(Sansevieria trifasciata)*
English Ivy *(Hedera helix)*
Money Tree *(Pachira aquatica)*
Rubber Plant *(Ficus elastica)*
Devil's Ivy *(Epipremnum aureum)*
Tail Flower *(Anthurium andraeanum)*
Tassel Fern *(Huperzia spp.)*

Full Moon
Fiddle-leaf Fig *(Ficus lyrata)*
Cast-Iron Plant *(Aspidistra elatior)*
Chain of Hearts *(Ceropegia woodii)*
Crown of Thorns *(Euphorbia milii)*
Desert Rose *(Adenium obesum)*
Zebra Plant *(Aphelandra squarrosa)*
Prayer Plant *(Maranta leuconeura)*
Umbrella Tree *(Schefflera arboricola)*
Moth Orchid *(Phalaenopsis spp.)*
Heart Leaf *(Philodendron hederaceum)*
Bird's Nest Fern *(Asplenium nidus)*
Spider Plant *(Chlorophytum comosum)*
Boston Fern *(Nephrolepis exaltata)*
Flaming Sword *(Vriesea splendens)*
Golden Cane Palm *(Dypsis lutescens)*

Hens and Chicks *(Sempervivum tectorum)*
Rainbow Pincushion *(Mammillaria rhodantha)*
Queen of Hearts *(Homalomena spp.)*

Waning Moon
Begonia *(Begonia spp.)*
Haworthia *(Haworthia spp.)*
Devil's Ivy *(Epipremnum aureum)*
Flaming Sword *(Vriesea splendens)*
Split Rock *(Pleiospilos nelii)*

New Moon
African Violet *(Saintpaulia spp.)*
Air Plant *(Tillandsia spp.)*
Peace Lily *(Spathiphyllum wallisii)*
Staghorn Fern *(Platycerium spp.)*
Venus Fly Trap *(Dionaea muscipula)*
Elephant Ear *(Alocasia x amazonica)*
Maidenhair Fern *(Adiantum raddianum)*
Painted Leaves *(Plectranthus scutellarioides)*
Split Rock *(Pleiospilos nelii)*

DEITIES AND THEIR HOUSEPLANTS

Aegina: Boston Fern *(Nephrolepis exaltata)*

Aine: Venus Fly Trap *(Dionaea muscipula)*

Aganyu: Haworthia *(Haworthia spp.)*

Amaterasu: Haworthia *(Haworthia spp.)*

Anaisa Pyé: Devil's Ivy *(Epipremnum aureum)*

Andraste: Hens and Chicks *(Sempervivum tectorum)*

Aphrodite: Fiddle-leaf Fig *(Ficus lyrata)*, Arrowhead Plant *(Syngonium podophyllum)*, Chain of Hearts *(Ceropegia woodii)*, Christmas Cactus *(Schlumbergera truncata)*, Desert Rose *(Adenium obesum)*, Heart Leaf *(Philodendron hederaceum)*, Venus Fly Trap *(Dionaea muscipula)*, Queen of Hearts *(Homalomena spp.)*

Ardat Lili: Money Tree *(Pachira aquatica)*

Artemis: African Violet *(Saintpaulias spp.)*, Bamboo Palm *(Rhapis excelsa)*, Umbrella Tree *(Schefflera arboricola)*, English Ivy *(Hedera helix)*

Astarte: Chain of Hearts *(Ceropegia woodii)*

Athena: African Violet *(Saintpaulia spp.)*, Arrowhead Plant *(Syngonium podophyllum)*

Azazel: Umbrella Tree *(Schefflera arboricola)*

Bacchus: English Ivy *(Hedera helix)*

Baku: Umbrella Tree *(Schefflera arboricola)*

Baldur: Aloe Vera *(Aloe barbadensis miller)*, Tassel Fern *(Huperzia spp.)*

Bast: Arrowhead Plant *(Syngonium podophyllum)*, Umbrella Tree *(Schefflera arboricola)*

Benten: Spider Plant *(Chlorophytum comosum)*

Blue Tara: Bird's Nest Fern *(Asplenium nidus)*, Elephant Ear *(Alocasia x amazonica)*

Brigit: Aloe Vera *(Aloe barbadensis miller)*, Arrowhead Plant *(Syngonium podophyllum)*, Tail Flower *(Anthurium andraeanum)*

Caboclo: Zebra Plant *(Aphelandra squarrosa)*

Chronos: Cast-Iron Plant *(Aspidistra elatior)*, Zebra Plant *(Aphelandra squarrosa)*

Chuku: Boston Fern *(Nephrolepis exaltata)*

Dainichi: Rainbow Pincushion *(Mammillaria rhodantha)*

Daphne: Umbrella Tree *(Schefflera arboricola)*

Demeter: Hens and Chicks *(Sempervivum tectorum)*

Diana: Prayer Plant *(Maranta leuconeura)*

Dionysos: Desert Rose *(Adenium obesum)*, English Ivy *(Hedera helix)*, Rubber Plant *(Ficus elastica)*

Durga: Haworthia *(Haworthia spp.)*, Golden Cane Palm *(Dypsis lutescens)*

E-bangishimog: Air Plant *(Tillandsia spp.)*

Eos: Arrowhead Plant *(Syngonium podophyllum)*

Elpis: Staghorn Fern *(Platycerium spp.)*

Ezili Freda Dahomey: Heart Leaf *(Philodendron hederaceum)*

Epona: Begonia *(Begonia spp.)*, Desert Rose *(Adenium obesum)*

Eros: Devil's Ivy *(Epipremnum aureum)*

Fu Lu Shou: Jade Plant *(Crassula ovata)*

Fortuna: Jade Plant *(Crassula ovata)*

Freya: Arrowhead Plant *(Syngonium podophyllum)*, Begonia *(Begonia spp.)*, Moth Orchid *(Phalaenopsis spp.)*

Frigg: African Violet *(Saintpaulia spp.)*

Gabriel: Staghorn Fern *(Platycerium spp.)*, Rainbow Pincushion *(Mammillaria rhodantha)*

Ganesha: Bamboo Palm *(Rhapis excelsa)*, Tail Flower *(Anthurium andraeanum)*

Gaia: Zebra Plant *(Aphelandra squarrosa)*, Prayer Plant *(Maranta leuconeura)*

Guadalupe: Rainbow Pincushion *(Mammillaria rhodantha)*, Queen of Hearts *(Homalomena spp.)*

Horus: Umbrella Tree *(Schefflera arboricola)*

Hanuman: Rubber Plant *(Ficus elastica)*

Hathor: Arrowhead Plant *(Syngonium podophyllum)*

Hekate: Snake Plant *(Sansevieria trifasciata)*, Haworthia *(Haworthia spp.)*, Devil's Ivy *(Epipremnum aureum)*, Tassel Fern *(Huperzia spp.)*

Hercules: Cast-Iron Plant *(Aspidistra elatior)*, Haworthia *(Haworthia spp.)*, Split Rock *(Pleiospilos nelii)*

Hermes: Air Plant *(Tillandsia spp.)*, Bamboo Palm *(Rhapis excelsa)*, Begonia *(Begonia spp.)*, Jade Plant *(Crassula ovata)*, Moth Orchid *(Phalaenopsis spp.)*

Hi'iaka: Devil's Ivy *(Epipremnum aureum)*

Hsi Wang Mu: Elephant Ear *(Alocasia x amazonica)*

Idunn: Cast-Iron Plant *(Aspidistra elatior)*

Iara: Christmas Cactus *(Schlumbergera truncata)*

Imana: Haworthia *(Haworthia spp.)*

Iris: Air Plant *(Tillandsia spp.)*, Prayer Plant *(Maranta leuconeura)*, Umbrella Tree *(Schefflera arboricola)*, Moth Orchid *(Phalaenopsis spp.)*, Rainbow Pincushion *(Mammillaria rhodantha)*

Isis: African Violet *(Saintpaulia spp.)*, Arrowhead Plant *(Syngonium podophyllum)*, Rubber Plant *(Ficus elastica)*

Itzamna: Arrowhead Plant *(Syngonium podophyllum)*

Ix Chel: Spider Plant *(Chlorophytum comosum)*

Jizo: Haworthia *(Haworthia spp.)*

Juno: Peace Lily *(Spathiphyllum wallisii)*, Rubber Plant *(Ficus elastica)*

Kali: Croton *(Codiaeum variegatum)*, Umbrella Tree *(Schefflera arboricola)*

Kanaloa: Croton *(Codiaeum variegatum)*

Kwoth: Boston Fern *(Nephrolepis exaltata)*, Split Rock *(Pleiospilos nelii)*

Krishna: Umbrella Tree *(Schefflera arboricola)*

Kuan Yin: Arrowhead Plant *(Syngonium podophyllum)*

Kwan Kung: Tail Flower *(Anthurium andraeanum)*

La Baleine: Umbrella Tree *(Schefflera arboricola)*

Sirène, La: Painted Leaves *(Plectranthus scutellarioides)*

Lakshmi: Arrowhead Plant *(Syngonium podophyllum)*, Jade Plant *(Crassula ovata)*, Money Tree *(Pachira aquatica)*, Golden Cane Palm *(Dypsis lutescens)*, Maidenhair Fern *(Adiantum raddianum)*

Lieu Hanh: Umbrella Tree *(Schefflera arboricola)*

Lilith: Begonia *(Begonia spp.)*

Mae Nak: Moth Orchid *(Phalaenopsis spp.)*

Maat: Zebra Plant *(Aphelandra squarrosa)*, Snake Plant *(Sansevieria trifasciata)*, Boston Fern *(Nephrolepis exaltata)*, Flaming Sword *(Vriesea splendens)*

Maneki Neko: Money Tree *(Pachira aquatica)*

Manitou: Venus Fly Trap *(Dionaea muscipula)*

Manjushri: Rubber Plant *(Ficus elastica)*

Maria Lionza: Maidenhair Fern *(Adiantum raddianum)*

Maximon: Money Tree *(Pachira aquatica)*

Medusa: Snake Plant *(Sansevieria trifasciata)*

Mercury: Moth Orchid *(Phalaenopsis spp.)*

Minerva: African Violet *(Saintpaulias spp.)*, Arrowhead Plant *(Syngonium podophyllum)*

Morrigan: Desert Rose *(Adenium obesum)*

Nanshe: Painted Leaves *(Plectranthus scutellarioides)*

Nike: Golden Cane Palm *(Dypsis lutescens)*

Njambi: Spider Plant *(Chlorophytum comosum)*

Njord: Air Plant *(Tillandsia spp.)*, Money Tree *(Pachira aquatica)*

Oba: Christmas Cactus *(Schlumbergera truncata)*

Ochosi: Umbrella Tree *(Schefflera arboricola)*

Odin: African Violet *(Saintpaulia spp.)*, Tail Flower *(Anthurium andraeanum)*

Ogun: Crown of Thorns *(Euphorbia milii)*, Snake Plant *(Sansevieria trifasciata)*,

Split Rock *(Pleiospilos nelii okuninushi):*
Money Tree *(Pachira aquatica)*
Omoikane: Staghorn Fern *(Platycerium
spp.)*
Orisha: Prayer Plant *(Maranta
leuconeura)*
Osiris: Aloe Vera *(Aloe barbadensis
miller),* English Ivy *(Hedera helix)*
Oshun: African Violet *(Saintpaulia
spp.),* Desert Rose *(Adenium obesum),*
Money Tree *(Pachira aquatica)*
Oshunmare: Maidenhair Fern
(Adiantum raddianum)
Oya: Croton *(Codiaeum variegatum),*
Snake Plant *(Sansevieria trifasciata)*
Pa Hsien: Umbrella Tree *(Schefflera
arboricola)*
Pan: Bamboo Palm *(Rhapis excelsa),*
Desert Rose *(Adenium obesum)*
Pandora: Staghorn Fern *(Platycerium
spp.)*
Parvati: Chain of Hearts *(Ceropegia
woodii)*
Pele: Arrowhead Plant *(Syngonium
podophyllum),* Chain of Hearts
(Ceropegia woodii),
Heart Leaf *(Philodendron hederaceum)*
Persephone: Aloe Vera *(Aloe barbadensis
miller)*
Pomona: Chain of Hearts *(Ceropegia
woodii),* Umbrella Tree *(Schefflera
arboricola)*
Poseidon: Air Plant *(Tillandsia spp.)*
Prometheus: Cast-Iron Plant
(Aspidistra elatior)
Proteus: Boston Fern *(Nephrolepis
exaltata)*

Quetzalcoatl: Air Plant *(Tillandsia
spp.),* Cast Iron Plant *(Aspidistra
elatior)*
Sabine: Hens and Chicks *(Sempervivum
tectorum)*
Sachamama: Tail Flower *(Anthurium
andraeanum)*
Saraswati: African Violet *(Saintpaulia
spp.),* Arrowhead Plant *(Syngonium
podophyllum),*
Zebra Plant *(Aphelandra squarrosa)*
Sequana: Bird's Nest Fern *(Asplenium
nidus)*
Shango: Flaming Sword *(Vriesea
splendens)*
Shichi Fukujin: Cast-Iron Plant
(Aspidistra elatior)
Shiva: Painted Leaves *(Plectranthus
scutellarioides)*
Sidhe: Air Plant *(Tillandsia spp.)*
Simbi: Snake Plant *(Sansevieria
trifasciata)*
Sirona: Tassel Fern *(Huperzia spp.)*
Spes: Staghorn Fern *(Platycerium spp.)*
Sukunahiko: Bird's Nest Fern
(Asplenium nidus)
Themis: Zebra Plant *(Aphelandra
squarrosa)*
Thor: Umbrella Tree *(Schefflera
arboricola),* Hens and Chicks
(Sempervivum tectorum)
Thoth: Prayer Plant *(Maranta
leuconeura)*
Ugajin: Bamboo Palm *(Rhapis excelsa)*
Venus: Fiddle-leaf Fig *(Ficus lyrata),*
Chain of Hearts *(Ceropegia woodii),*

Christmas Cactus *(Schlumbergera truncata)*, Desert Rose *(Adenium obesum)*,
Heart Leaf *(Philodendron hederaceum)*, Venus Fly Trap *(Dionaea muscipula)*,
Queen of Hearts *(Homalomena spp.)*
Victoria: Hens and Chicks *(Sempervivum tectorum)*
Weaving Maiden: Spider Plant *(Chlorophytum comosum)*

White Tara: Prayer Plant *(Maranta leuconeura)*
Xochipilli: Chain of Hearts *(Ceropegia woodii)*, Snake Plant *(Sansevieria trifasciata)*
Zeus: Air Plant *(Tillandsia spp.)*, Aloe Vera *(Aloe barbadensis miller)*, Crown of Thorns *(Euphorbia milii)*

EPIPHYLLUM TRUNCATUM

²/₃ Nat. size

PL. 118

GENERAL HOUSEPLANT CARE

ANYONE CAN GARDEN INDOORS

Gardening is a learned skill and, like any skill, the more you practise it, the better you become at it. Some people may have a natural affinity for it, and they are usually known as having a 'Green Thumb' but I believe there is no such thing as the opposite: a 'Brown (or Black) Thumb'.

Everyone experiences accidents, mistakes, and even disasters, in gardening. It is an organic undertaking and, as such, the outcomes are also organic. To grow a Green Thumb takes time, dedication and practice, but anyone can do it!

Gardening indoors has its own challenges. If you are new to gardening, then select a few of the plants in this book labelled 'easy', to get you started. Those plants noted as more challenging to grow just need more care, additional attention and perhaps are more finicky in their requirements; but they are not beyond the capabilities of beginner gardeners who have the time and motivation to invite these plants into their lives.

When purchasing plants, gather all information. Do not throw away any tags or labels that come with them; explore further by asking staff for tips and reading through gardening books and online resources.

GARDEN JOURNALING

Keeping a gardening journal is an excellent way of storing your information on the plant together and following the progress of your plant. I like to set my gardening journals in the following way (which might give you some inspiration to start your own):

Numbering

Number each page on the outer bottom corner. This makes looking up your information easier once your journal becomes full.

Contents

Leave the first one or two pages free to add a list of the contents of your journal with its page numbers, as you create.

Entries

Just like gardening, I'm pretty organic with my entries, but I usually dedicate four pages, in an A5-sized journal, to each plant. I will note the date of purchase/propagation, any tag will be taped in, or I'll transcribe it, and growing notes. This will usually take up a page, and because I love botanical history and ethnobotany, I will add another page of these notes and will sketch the plant. You might like to do the same or add a small photo. The next two pages are left for diary notes about the plant or anything I might like to add in the future.

INDOOR GARDENING TOOLS

As you would imagine, indoor gardening tools are smaller than their outdoor cousins, but they need to be looked after in the same way. Keep them all together in a box, bag or on a shelf. Clean after each use and most should last a lifetime.

Gloves

These protect your hands from dirt, irritants and toxic materials. You should have at least two pairs, one general canvas type for everyday dry tasks, and another that are waterproof for wet tasks. Wash regularly to prevent cross contamination.

Watering Cans

Two are usually required. A larger one of at least 4 litres (1 gallon) when you are mixing up large amounts of fertiliser and watering larger plants. A smaller watering can that holds about one to three cups of water is very handy to water smaller plants and to direct water to specific areas in pots. Empty after each use and wash with mild detergent and rinse if any substances have been used in them.

Mister

This is essential for many indoor plants because it will help you increase the humidity that these plants require. Misters are sealed units and can be left with water in them.

Secateurs

Pruning, clipping and cutting are all easiest with a good pair of secateurs. Better quality ones will last a lifetime and not let you down. Left-handed models are available and so are smaller handles for people, like me, who have small hands. Wash after each use using a dishwashing type brush (only used for your gardening tools) and a mild detergent. Dry with a soft cloth and allow to air dry further by leaving open. Once dry, lubricate and protect with a very fine spray of vegetable oil. Sharpen regularly on a sharpening stone.

Knife

A small sharp knife is essential for propagation and smaller trimming tasks. Wash after each use, with a mild detergent. Dry with a soft cloth. Sharpen regularly on a sharpening stone.

Hand Trowel

Used to dig, to fill pots, to aerate soil, and to help move plants when transplanting. These are available in plastic or metal. For durability, choose a non-rusting metal type. Wash after each use with a dishwashing type brush (only used for your gardening tools) and a mild detergent. Dry with a soft cloth.

Brush

A paintbrush or cooking basting brush is very helpful for removing dirt and debris from fragile plants, succulents and cactus.

Aerator

Plants often need their soil loosened to allow for air and drainage. Although there are metal, plastic and wooden aerators available, any slim strong stick can be used for the task, such as a small bamboo stake or chopstick.

Hand Fork

Hand forks are also handy for aerating, transplanting, and for mixing soil blends. Hand forks are available in plastic, or metal for longevity. Wash after each use with a dishwashing type brush (only used for your gardening tools) and a mild detergent. Dry with a soft cloth.

Stakes

Many plants need staking for support, and it's a good idea to have a few handy – any plant can suddenly need a little help standing up. Usual materials are wood, plastic or metal. I like to use wood (bamboo in a range of sizes to suit).

Ties

These will help secure plants to stakes and can be found in plastic, metal, plastic-covered metal, or you could use twine.

HELP YOUR PLANTS THRIVE

Plants may adapt to many conditions and stay alive, but to have healthy, thriving and lush houseplants that are happy, you need to give them the environment that best matches their origins. To do this, light, temperature, water and food requirements need to be met. Diseases and pests will also be something to watch for and attend to.

Care Problems

HOW MUCH LIGHT?
Problems that may be light related:
thin, straggly growth: not enough light
leaf drop: too much light
leaf wilt: too much light, too much heat
yellow foliage: too much light
burnt foliage: too much light, too much heat
brown upper leaf surface: too much light

WHAT TEMPERATURE?
Problems that may be temperature related:
wilting plant: temperature too high
yellow foliage: temperature too low
bud drop: temperature too low
small leaves: temperature too high
deformed leaves: temperature too high or too low
fast, uneven growth: temperature too high or too low

HOW MUCH WATER?
Problems that may be water related:
leaf drop: under- or over-watering

leaf curl: under- or over-watering
brown leaf edges: low humidity, under-watering
red leaves: under-watering
rotting roots: over-watering, pot sitting in water
soil not retaining water: quality of soil is poor
bud drop: under-watering
no flowers: under-watering
corky patches (oedema): over-watering

HOW MUCH FOOD?

Problems that may be feeding related:
new leaves are yellow with green veins: low iron
pale leaves: under-feeding
small leaves with yellow edges: phosphorus deficiency
slow growth: under-feeding
bottom leaves have yellow/brown edges: phosphorus deficiency
brown leaf tips: over-feeding
few or no flowers: under-feeding

COMMON DISEASES

Damping Off

seedlings collapse and die and a white growth on soil is present

Remove any covering and provide adequate ventilation for those parts of the plant that are still alive. There is usually no saving dead seedlings.

Downy Mildew

unnatural coloured patches, a mouldy growth on underside of leaves and leaf drop

All affected parts of the plant (even the whole plant if extensive) need to be removed and thrown in the rubbish bin (do not compost). Wetting leaves when watering can cause the problem. Avoid doing this to prevent spread and reoccurrence.

Fungal Leaf Spot

leaves display dark spots ringed in yellow edges

Remove affected foliage and bin. Treat plant with a fungicide and increase ventilation and airflow around your plant.

Grey Mould

fuzzy grey growth on foliage, and decay

Work quickly as grey mould kills plants fast. Remove affected foliage and bin. Treat plant with a fungicide and increase ventilation and airflow around your plant.

Powdery Mildew

white fluffy growth on any part of the plant

This disease is often caused by poor ventilation and over-watering. Treat with a fungicide and improve conditions for the plant. To avoid, ensure good airflow and spacing between plants and make sure you are not over-watering.

Root Rot

wilting plant that seems not to revive when watered

Caused by letting plant become completely dried out for a long period or by continual over-watering. There is no cure, so plant and soil will need to be thrown away in a rubbish bin, to prevent fungus spreading, and pot washed well.

Rust

small rust-coloured growths on the underside of leaves

There is no cure and you must remove affected leaves, and sometimes whole plants, and bin to prevent spread. Caused by over-feeding, so reduce in future.

Sooty Mould

Black and sometimes charcoal- or dark-brown growth on leaves

This is a fungus that grows on the honeydew that some pests leave behind. Wash off the fungus with warm water and treat the plant to rid it of pests such as aphids, which are the likely cause.

Stem and Crown Rot

Around the base of a plant stems turn brown and black and this travels up the plant

It is a fungus caused by over-watering and inadequate drainage. Usually fatal. Plant and growing medium should be removed and pot cleaned.

Viruses

Yellow, white or green stripes, spots, streaks or mosaic patterns, or distorted growth

Cause could be a virus, and for this there will be no cure. Bin plant and soil and clean pot.

COMMON PESTS

Aphids

Small black or green insects found, particularly, on new growth.

Solution: In a spray bottle, add a solution of neem oil, or make up 1 cup of water to 2 teaspoons of mild dishwashing detergent. Spray the affected areas to remove the aphids.

Spider Mite

Tiny sap-sucking insects too small for the eye to see. The leaves will lose colour and become mottled.

Solution: Remove all affected parts of the plant and place in the rubbish bin. Mist rest of the plant with water, which deters spider mite. Heavy infestations may require a pesticide.

Thrips

Very tiny winged insects that are 2mm ($12/16$") in length. They cause dullness in leaves, and silver patches with tiny black dots.

Solution: Pesticide or sticky traps.

Earwigs

Small brown crawling insects up to 1.5cm (½") in length, with pincers on their rear end.

Solution: They are nocturnal. Remove if they appear.

Leafhoppers

Tiny green jumping insects about 3mm ($1/8$") in length. They cause mottling of the leaf colour.

*Solution:*Although pesticides can be used, leafhoppers do not cause damage to plants and can be left alone.

Scale Insects

They appear as tiny bumps and scales of about 1cm ($\frac{1}{2}$") in length.

Solution: A mixture of ¼ cup mild detergent with a tablespoon of methylated spirits can be brushed on the affected areas. This can damage some plants, so you would be advised to test first on a small area. Leave for a few days to see results. Other methods are to remove affected foliage and bin.

Caterpillars, Slugs and Snails

Not usually a problem for indoor plants and are usually brought in from a larger garden setting when introducing your plant indoors.

Solution: Remove if they appear.

HOUSEPLANT CARE RECIPES

Neem Pesticide

- 2 cups water
- 1 teaspoon mild dishwashing liquid
- 2 teaspoons neem oil

Mix together water, dishwashing liquid and neem oil in a spray bottle.
Best used by spraying on affected plant areas on particularly sunny days.
Can be used daily until infestation has been eliminated.

Chilli Pesticide

- 2 cups water
- ½ teaspoon mild dishwashing liquid
- ½ tablespoon chilli powder

Mix together water, dishwashing liquid and chilli powder in a spray bottle.
Best used by spraying on affected plant areas on particularly sunny days.
Can be used daily until infestation has been eliminated.

Oil & Soda Fungicide

- 4 cups water
- ½ teaspoon mild dishwashing liquid
- ½ teaspoon vegetable oil
- 2 teaspoons bicarbonate of soda (baking soda)

Mix together water, dishwashing liquid, oil and soda in a spray bottle.
Best used by spraying on affected plant areas on particularly sunny days.
Can be used daily until fungus has been eliminated.

BOTANICAL GLOSSARY

aerial roots: roots of a plant that form and live above the ground

angiosperms: flowering plants

bract: a modified leaf

cultivar: a plant produced through selective breeding

cutting: a piece of a plant that is used in propagation

division: separating a plant into more plants

dormancy: a period when little or no growth occurs

epiphyte: a plant that grows on and/or obtains its nutrients from another plant

ericaceous: slightly acidic

foliar: relating to leaves, or for leaves

frond: a leaf or leaf-like part of a palm, fern or similar plant

honeydew: a sugar-rich sticky secretion produced by aphids and other sap sucking insects

hybrid: the result of cross-pollinating two different plant varieties

leaf lobes: distinct protrusions, either rounded or pointed, on the edges of a leaf

necrotic leaf spot: dark spots that indicate a plant is under distress

node: where a leaf attaches to the stem

offset: a small, almost complete, child plant that has been naturally produced from its parent plant

perlite: a form of obsidian consisting of glassy globules in plant-growth media

petiole: like a petal

plantlet: young or small plant

propagate: the process of breeding a plant by natural processes, from the parent plant

re-pot: put a plant into another pot, usually larger

root ball: the main mass of roots at the base of a plant

root-bound: when the roots that grow of a plant have no room to expand in their container

spadix: a spike of tiny flowers closely arranged round a fleshy axis

spathe: a large sheathing bract enclosing the flower cluster of some plants

spent: dead

sphagnum moss: a type of natural moss that has excellent water holding attributes

succulent: a plant having thick fleshy leaves or stems adapted to storing water

suckers: a plant growth that grows from the base of the root of the plant at a certain distance away from the plant

taproot: the primary descending root of a plant

terminal: situated at the tip or apex

variegation: patterns and multiple colours on plants

vermiculite: a mineral that improves the drainage of soils

BIBLIOGRAPHY

Coombes, Allen J., *Dictionary of Plant Names* (Timber Press 2002)

Graves, Julia, *The Language of Plants* (Lindisfarne Books 2012)

Harrison, Lorraine, *RHS Latin for Gardeners* (Mitchell Beazley 2012)

Hemphill, John & Rosemary, *Myths and Legends of the Garden* (Hodder & Stoughton 1997)

Oxley, B. C. (Jerry); Allen, Sheila; Stackhouse, Shirley *Complete Guide to Indoor Plants* (Reader's Digest 1980)

Pavord, Anna, *The Naming of Names: The Search for Order in the World of Plants* (Bloomsbury 2005)

Vickery, Roy, *A Dictionary of Plant-Lore* (Oxford University Press 1995)

White, Ian, *Australian Bush Flower Healing* (Bantam Books 1999)

ABOUT THE AUTHOR

Cheralyn Darcey is a naturalist, botanical alchemist, eco artist, organic gardener, sustainable florist and the author of over a dozen books and oracle decks dedicated to the study of the connections between plants and humans. Cheralyn is a popular guest on national television and radio, and a presenter at international festivals, libraries, museums and gardening events, where she shares the botanical history, ancient magick and folklore of our gardens and plants, to inspire renewed care for our land and helping others find personal guidance and inspiration in nature.

Her artwork has been featured in galleries and art prizes across Australia and the USA, including The Australian Museum and the Manly Art Gallery. Cheralyn was an Environmental Artist in Residence during the International Conference of Eco Ideas in 2011, and has a long association with many environmental organisations, creating eco artworks, educational workshops and presentations, as well as working as an administration- and field volunteer.

Cheralyn is a regular guest on the morning television show *Studio Ten*, as their botanical expert. Her organic vegetable, and magickal herb and flower gardens have been featured in many publications including *Good Organic Gardening* magazine, and she has been interviewed by, and written for other print media, including *The Sydney Morning Herald*, *The Daily Telegraph*, many regional newspapers, *ABC Gardening Australia*, *Air Asia Inflight*, *Country Style*, *Harper's Bazaar* and *Elle*.

www.cheralyndarcey.com

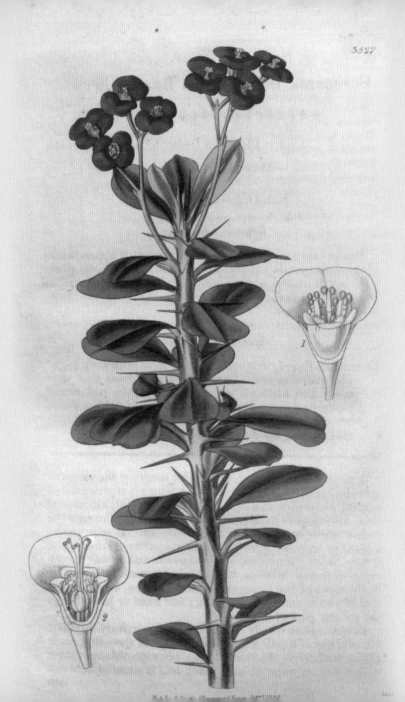